W9-AHK-383

A Treasury of
Ohio Tales

A Treasury of Ohio Tales

Webb Garrison

RUTLEDGE HILL PRESS
Nashville, Tennessee

Copyright © 1993 Webb Garrison

All rights reserved. Written permission must be secured from the publisher to use or reproduce any part of this book, except for brief quotations in critical reviews or articles.

Published in Nashville, Tennessee, by Rutledge Hill Press, Inc., 211 Seventh Avenue North, Nashville, Tennessee 37219.

Typography: D&T/Bailey Typesetting, Inc., Nashville, Tennessee

Library of Congress Cataloging-in-Publication Data

Garrison, Webb B.
    A treasury of Ohio tales / Webb Garrison.
      p. cm.
    Includes index.
    ISBN 1-55853-249-8
    1. Ohio—History—Anecdotes. I. Title.
F491.6.G36 1993   93-29073
977.1—dc20   CIP

Printed in the United States of America
  2 3 4 5 6 7—98 97 96 95 94

Contents

Middle America in Geography Only

Far from being average or just in the middle, Ohio ranks at or close to the top among our fifty states in many respects. If Virginia is "the mother of presidents," Ohio has to be the father. Ulysses S. Grant was first in a seldom-broken line of chief executives that extended for more than half a century: Rutherford B. Hayes, James A. Garfield, Benjamin Harrison, William McKinley, William Howard Taft, and Warren G. Harding.

No other state has a heritage quite like that of "New Connecticut." Launched far from a seat of government, the Western Reserve was destined to be crossed by the National Road—of which many outside the Buckeye State have never heard.

Since many colorful and influential persons have strong Ohio ties, it is impossible to deal with more than a fraction of them in a small book. Many significant achievers were reluctantly pushed aside after reams of source material about them had been gathered.

Every man and woman finally selected for inclusion here has a vivid and interesting story. Although some made no significant and lasting national impact, each is unique in his or her own way. Several U.S. presidents are conspicuous by their absence. Their deeds may have been monumental, but by comparison with Lottie Moon and William C. Quantrill, their lives were prosaic or even dull. Other notable Buckeyes such as the Wright brothers and Neil Armstrong have been

7

reluctantly omitted because their stories are universally familiar. In the case of Buckeyes whose names and achievements are familiar everywhere, I've tried to focus upon a little-known or unusual aspect.

It has been both a challenging and a rewarding experience to delve into Ohio lore and to share a small part of it with readers. This volume could not have been produced without the significant aid of many persons. Some of those who gave notable assistance with source material and/or illustrations are:

Marian Davies, Akron-Summit County Public Library; Kimberly A. Keiser, Champion International Corporation; Laurence J. Russell, the Edison Birthplace Association; public relations department, Goodyear Tire & Rubber Co.; Mary Maker, Martins Ferry Public Library; C. Martin Miller and Beth Weaver, Miami University; Brad Nixon, NCR Corporation; Michael Johnson, Ohio Baseball Hall of Fame; Ruth A. Meyer, the Harriet Beecher Stowe House; Superintendent Kurt C. Topham, William Howard Taft Historic Site; Cate O'Hara, the Taft Museum; Margaret M. Bonamico, Trumpet in the Land; Gina Merrill, Tuscarawas County Public Library; Carol Willsey Bell, Warren-Trumbull County Public Library; and the staff of the reference division, Western Reserve Historical Society.

Here's hoping that you'll have fun in these pages—and maybe also learn a little, painlessly!

—Webb Garrison, Fall 1993

PART ONE

Memorable First Events and Achievements

The first naval victory on inland waters won by colonials fighting the British was on Lake Erie. The first interstate highway financed by the U.S. Congress was originally planned to terminate at the Ohio River.

Neil Armstrong was the first man to walk on the moon, and John Glenn is the first former astronaut to become a member of the U.S. Senate. Wilbur and Orville Wright were first to fly in a heavier-than-air machine. Charles Kettering was first to equip an automobile with a self-starter.

Cincinnati was the first city to achieve world prominence as a pork processing center. Akron is first among all cities as headquarters for rubber corporations.

Procter & Gamble made Cincinnati "the soap capital of the world," while the National Cash Register Company made Dayton the first U.S. city from which a big overseas market for manufactured goods was established.

If space permitted, this list could go on and on. From dozens of contenders, half a dozen Buckeyes who were first in a field of endeavor are described in the following chapters.

Thomas Edison as he appeared in 1892 after having discovered "the Edison effect" that led to the electronic age. [LIBRARY OF CONGRESS]

1

Edison Took the First Fumbling Step Toward the Electronic Age

"The tiny 'electrical sun' is ready—just as it was fifty years ago. But questions remain. Will it light? Will it remain lighted for any length of time?

"Stand by, ladies and gentlemen, as Thomas Alva Edison prepares to connect wires. We shall see, in just an instant.

"*It flickers! Now it glows steadily! The electric light is a reality! The Golden Jubilee of the electrical sun is here!*"

Glued to radio sets, Americans everywhere were reliving in 1929 an 1879 drama when Thomas Edison had tested his most recent electric light bulb and pronounced it to be a success. However, the ceremonies being held fifty years later were at Henry Ford's Greenfield Village rather than at Edison's laboratory.

Just a few years after the incandescent bulb was pronounced a commercial success, the General Electric Company had acquired control of it, with only the Westinghouse Company offering challenging competition. Now both giant manufacturers were under assault in Congress. Though long dead, Senator John Sherman of Ohio, brother of the Civil War general, had set in motion the events that put Michigan center stage for what was billed as a gigantic tribute to the inventor born in Milan, Ohio.

As the fiftieth anniversary of Edison's most triumphant moment approached, General Electric officials began making plans to celebrate in Schenectady. Publicity linked with the Jubilee of Light might remove some of the pressure created by charges that the corporation had a monopoly on products of the inventor's brain. Concepts behind the Sherman Anti-

Trust Act and the laws derived from it threatened to cause real trouble. With many homes still not wired for electricity, the celebration might also bring about a rise in sales.

Plans for an October 21 jubilee were still in the formative stage when Henry Ford learned from an Edison employee what was being planned for Schenectady. This leak turned the auto manufacturer into "a dynamo of energy." Soon he walked, unannounced, into Edison's workplace. Legend says he muttered, "I'll show the bastards; I'll bring the party to Michigan!"

It was easy to persuade Thomas Edison that the corporation growing rich from his inventions planned to take advantage of him. So he may have suggested that the site of the jubilee be changed. Apparently he failed to remember that his friend from Michigan was almost ready to open his own museum as well as Greenfield Village.

Whatever the chain of circumstances that led to the decision to celebrate with Ford, Edison exhibited his uncommonly stubborn self once it was announced. Come hell or high water, he would not be in Schenectady on October 21.

Triumphant, Ford re-created much of Edison's Menlo Park laboratory and plant and added for an awed public a reproduction of the train of the Grand Trunk Railway with its baggage car displaying young Tom Edison's rolling laboratory.

Led by President and Mrs. Herbert Hoover, notables converged upon Greenfield Village. To heighten the drama, Mr. and Mrs. Ford and Mr. and Mrs. Edison met the Hoovers outside Detroit. There all six stepped into a tiny old-fashioned railway car drawn by a wood-burning locomotive of Civil War vintage.

Hours after having reached the site of the jubilee, Thomas Edison rolled up his sleeves and re-enacted a watershed moment in modern life. By creating a vacuum inside a glass bulb holding a spiral of carbonized sewing thread, he turned on the current. After flickering very briefly, the "electrical sun" glowed brightly and steadily.

Neither the notables present for the jubilee nor the radio listeners were told that Edison's chief success had been commercial rather than scientific. At least two decades before the lights came on at Menlo Park, an English physicist had used a carbon filament in a light bulb. Learning that air inside a bulb would have to be nearly or entirely exhausted if the filament was to last, Sir Joseph Wilson began putting tiny strips of burned paper within evacuated bulbs at least as early as 1848.

Wilson was making significant progress by 1860 and eventually learned how to produce the high vacuum desired. Swan lamps illuminated the House of Commons in 1881 and quickly became standard in many British cities. But Edison was far more active in gaining patents than was Sir Joseph. The two men jousted briefly in England, then settled their differences out of court and in 1883 formed a joint corporation.

Neither at the 1929 Jubilee of Light nor later has the American public been widely informed that Thomas Edison was not the first person to develop a functional electric light.

Seventh and youngest child of a Canadian descended from an American who served under Lord Howe during the Revolutionary War, Tom Edison was born in Milan, Ohio, fourteen years before the Civil War began. When the family

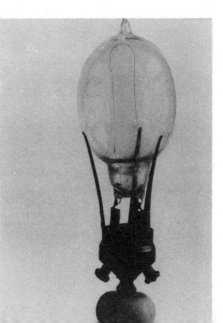

After hundreds of unsuccessful attempts, Edison produced a long-lived electric bulb by using platinum lead-in wires and carbonized thread as the filament in a vacuum. [EDISON BIRTHPLACE MUSEUM]

Built in 1841, Edison's birthplace was purchased by him in 1906 but was not wired for electricity until 1927. [EDISON BIRTHPLACE MUSEUM]

moved to Port Huron, Michigan, Tom started to school, but his teachers found him uncooperative and quickly labeled him "addled." After a few months his frustrated mother taught him at home most of the meager "book learning" he absorbed in childhood. Soon, however, there was what he called a chemical laboratory in the Edison house. To prevent damage from meddlesome siblings and neighbors, he put homemade labels reading "Poison" on most vials and bottles.

Although his father's grain and lumber business was prospering, young Edison couldn't wait to start earning his own money. He published and sold a tiny newspaper; then he set up shop on a train, where he expanded his line to include candy and tobacco. Tolerant railroaders permitted him to use part of a baggage car as a chemical laboratory, which no one then could foresee would later be re-created at Greenfield Village.

Once when a young Edison was possibly in danger of falling under a moving train, the young entrepreneur was seized by a brakeman who yanked him aboard by the head. That narrow escape may have contributed to premature deafness, which helped to direct the course of his life.

At age fifteen, Tom snatched a small boy from the path of an approaching train. Unable to reward him with cash, the boy's father offered to teach the rescuer telegraphy. Very soon, Edison found he could hear the click of a telegraph instrument more distinctly than voices or other sounds. So without giving up his laboratory experiments, he concentrated upon his new skill and became "the best and fastest telegrapher in the business."

In 1868 he went to Boston to take a job as a telegrapher. Believing New York offered greater opportunities, he went there to find employment. He was in a line waiting to be interviewed when a broker's telegraph machine failed. Edison quickly repaired it and was given a much better job than he had hoped to find.

The shouts of employees within the brokerage firm as they called out stock prices bothered him so much that he set out to eliminate them. Soon he had a crude but workable stock ticker for which he wished to get as much as $5,000. He presented it to the head of a firm, suggested that he'd consider an offer, and was amazed to receive $40,000.

Edison is most widely remembered for the commercial success of his light bulb, but his most innovative work was done with sound. Western Union Telegraph Company officials felt that there might be a future in the telephone, but they didn't know how to use it in their operations. To send messages effectively, engineers believed it would be necessary to find a way to record at the receiving end.

Tinfoil might do the job, Edison reasoned, but waxed paper would be much cheaper and might work as well. On July 5, 1877, he wrote one of his many terse memos to himself: "For autographic Tel write your message in parafined paper & transmit by a spring contact." It was this crude initial work on "a telephone speaker" that led to the phonograph.

Characteristically, while still experimenting with waxed paper bands, disks, and metallic foil wrapped around cylinders, he filed patent application #141. Before he achieved success, he prepared a press release to announce it. Referring to himself as Mr. Edison, the Electrician, he was ready to tell the world that eager buyers would soon find available "an apparatus for recording automatically the human voice and reproducing it at any desired time in the future."

In the life of the Ohio native, imagination and hope always bounced far ahead of reality. Without having produced a single functional phonograph, he predicted:

> I will use the principle to make dolls speak or sing or cry. It can also be applied to toy dogs and fowls, and to whistles and toy steam engines. Orchestral and vocal music can be preserved, so that a family with one machine and 1,000 sheets of music can have endless entertainment.

Thomas Edison was awarded over one thousand patents, and some authorities estimate that more than half of them were results of his deafness, which led to his absorbing interest in sounds.

Numerous present-day professional research workers, holders of doctorates from noted universities, tend to scorn Thomas Edison as "an inspired tinker." His tangible results, they charge, were produced by driving himself and his employees almost to the breaking point, trying one thing after another until he stumbled upon a workable device or substance.

Such a view of Edison's career overlooks an 1883 achievement. Had they been asked, trained physicists such as Sir Joseph Wilson and his colleagues could have explained the nature of the matter of the universe, though Edison could not. According to them, the smallest unit of material was a molecule. Existence of electrons was not yet known.

Working to extend the life of his direct-current light bulbs, Edison was puzzled to discover that they became blackened in use. Clearly, heat that made a filament glow also caused tiny particles of carbon to bounce toward surrounding glass. For reasons unknown, only the negative leg of the filament created this phenomenon.

Since carbon particles that jumped from the filament to the glass might carry an electrical charge, he added an additional

Edison after five continuous days and nights of work upon the phonograph.
[EDISON BIRTHPLACE MUSEUM]

experimental pole—or positively charged electrode—to some bulbs. If it was operated in a vacuum, he found that in such a bulb current flowed without wires. Therefore, on November 15, 1883, he filed a patent for "a voltage regulator using a bulb with two electrodes."

When patent #307,031 was awarded to him, no one pretended to understand the physical process that was involved. Not until decades later was "the Edison effect lamp" recognized to be the world's first electronic instrument. Later it was found to operate by generating free electrons whose movements were controlled.

Today the man who was not first to develop a workable electric light is recognized around the world as having discovered the effects that brought the electronic age into existence.

The Edison Birthplace Museum at Milan displays many memorabilia; for information call (419) 499-2135.

2

Big Bill and Nellie Taft Were First in Many Ways

"There's no way on earth that we can use the east portico of the Capitol. You will begin your administration by setting a record—taking the oath during the worst blizzard, ever, for this ceremony," Major Archibald Butts informed the president-elect on March 4, 1909.

"Then we'll use the Senate chamber," responded the largest man to win the nation's highest office. "Nellie— Mrs. Taft that is—can ride back to the house in the carriage with me."

"That has never been done—"

"No matter; you may see a good many things change, Major. Let's get on with the inauguration. I always said it would be a mighty cold day when I got to be president!"

Get on with it they did, on a day so foul that ice-laden trees toppled and prevented many trains from entering Washington. William Howard Taft did not at the moment realize it, but his spontaneous response to his personal aide proved to be prophetic. For the first time since the Civil War, the inaugural address—delivered to a handful of dignitaries who braved the cold—dealt directly with the mounting problem of race relations.

That night the new chief executive scored another first. Weighing about 330 pounds, he proved entirely too big for the White House bathtub. When Archibald Butts learned of the dilemma, he smiled quietly and telephoned a business friend. "J. L. Mott Iron Works makes an oversize model," he informed Taft. "Instead of the usual pieces of furniture, that tub will be the first thing to be installed for the new tenants of this place."

As the incoming chief executive, Taft scored a "first" in terms of the worst weather, ever, for an inauguration. [AUTHOR'S COLLECTION]

When the enormous bathtub arrived, four staff members crawled into it, smiling broadly to be photographed. Before the photographer left, the president and Mrs. Taft posed for him with their son, Robert, a future senator.

When Taft was born at Mount Auburn, the suburban development lay well past the boundaries of Cincinnati. Today the National Historic Site that includes his boyhood home is on Auburn Avenue, not far from Christ Hospital.

From early childhood, the boy, whom playmates called Big Lug, knew that he was expected to become a third-generation attorney. Never questioning or swerving, he was admitted to the bar at age twenty-two. Having been a part-time reporter for the Cincinnati *Commercial* while studying law, he was offered $1,500 a year for full-time work. Without hesitation, he shook his head. "Thank you, but I prefer to become assistant prosecutor of Hamilton County at $1,200," he said.

His 1886 marriage to Helen Herron, whom he always called Nellie, brought two wealthy and influential families together. Soon Governor Joseph B. Foraker invited him to fill an unexpired term as judge of the Cincinnati Superior Court.

Punch, *the British humor magazine, derided Taft as having been "fixed up" by Roosevelt to look exactly like him.* [PUNCH (JUNE 17, 1908)]

Having acquired the nickname that stuck to him for the rest of his life, Big Bill accepted eagerly. Nellie and his parents already knew that more than anything else in the world he hoped someday to become a justice of the U.S. Supreme Court; this would be one short step toward his goal.

Soon after starting a full term to which he had been elected, Ohio influence in Washington paid off. President Benjamin Harrison appointed the man from Cincinnati a judge of the sixth circuit of the newly established U.S. Circuit Court of Appeals. Eight years later, another Buckeye chief executive, William McKinley, chose him to head a commission to phase out the military government in the Philippines. Taft moved so rapidly that on July 4, 1901, he became the first civil governor of the Pacific islands, ceded to the United States after the Spanish-American War.

Because his high post required him to confer frequently with the president, Taft became a trusted adviser and then an intimate friend of Theodore Roosevelt. Political insiders, however, predicted that the friendship would not last because the governor of the Philippines was a likely candidate for the White House.

Ignoring the pundits, Roosevelt became so fond of Taft that he repeatedly offered to nominate him for the Supreme Court. Nothing would have pleased the big man better, but Nellie already had her eye on the presidency. Her father had been a college classmate of Benjamin Harrison and a law partner of Rutherford B. Hayes. As a result, Nellie—a frequent house guest in the White House—at age seventeen announced that she intended one day to be mistress of the place.

When Roosevelt picked Nellie's husband as his successor, cartoonists ridiculed Big Bill as an identical twin of the Rough Rider. That didn't prevent the Republican National Convention from nominating him on the first ballot in June 1908. In a heated contest with noted orator William Jennings Bryan, Taft won by more than 1,300,000 votes.

Correctly regarding herself as instrumental in pushing her husband to seek the presidency, on the day of his inauguration Nellie didn't hesitate to break with established precedent by riding in the presidential carriage. Soon she launched the first public project ever sponsored by a First Lady: erection of a bandstand at the foot of an elliptical drive that ran through Potomac Park.

Then she scored another triumph. Extremely fond of Japanese cherry trees, she scoured nurseries to find and plant 80 trees along the banks of the Potomac River. Later an additional 2,000 trees reached her from Tokyo. Mrs. Theodora Ozaki, wife of the Japanese mayor, wrote Nellie Taft that the gift leading to the cherry blossom festivals of later decades was "sent as a memorial of national friendship between Japan

Big Bill, Nellie, and their son Robert soon after taking up residence at 1600 Pennsylvania Avenue. [LIBRARY OF CONGRESS]

and the United States." Found to be infected with a fungus, the trees were burned but were replaced by 3,000 more whose planting began on March 27, 1912, under the direction of Mrs. Taft. In 1914 she became the first wife of a president to write a book issued by a commercial publisher, *Recollections of Full Years.*

While Nellie was filling the nation's capital with beautiful sights and sounds, her husband was repeatedly saying that "the presidency isn't all it is cracked up to be." To intimates he explained, "When I hear someone say 'Mr. President,' I look around expecting to see Roosevelt." By the time he became comfortable as master of the White House, he was in the habit of complaining that "the major part of the president's role is to increase the gate receipts of expositions and fairs and bring tourists into the town."

In the presidential election of 1912, Taft, the Republican Party candidate, lost votes to his predecessor, Theodore Roosevelt, who ran as a third-party candidate, a Progressive. Democrat Woodrow Wilson was elected.

Privately delighted to leave 1600 Pennsylvania Avenue after just four years, Taft looked back upon his tenure with considerable satisfaction. For the first time, he had insisted that it is a function of the president to present Congress with a proposed budget. Formerly, heads of departments acted independently and without coordination with colleagues. Along with many lawmakers, they opposed the notion of a single federal budget and managed to block passage of the act Taft sponsored.

Still, he did something few modern presidents have done: during four years he trimmed the national debt by about $25,000,000. During the debt-ridden 1990s, language establishing his 1910 Commission on Economy and Efficiency seems almost surreal. Having inherited an annual deficit of $58,000,000, he accumulated a surplus of $86,000,000 before leaving office.

During periods of wrestling with budgets and the national debt, subsequent chief executives have had reason to remember that it was William Howard Taft who made the president personally responsible for these areas. He did it from

Though he seldom scored below 115, Taft valiantly stuck to golf as the game's first presidential devotee. [GEORGE G. BAIN PHOTO, 1909]

work space that he transformed into what he called the Oval Office, something unheard of in the White House until his administration.

Big Bill was the first chief executive to keep automobiles at 1600 Pennsylvania Avenue. Of the four he personally owned, his favorite—perhaps because of its size—was a gigantic seven-passenger White Steamer built in Cleveland by the White Sewing Machine Company.

In spite of the fact that he found it impossible to stoop low enough to place a golf ball on a tee, Taft was the first presidential golfer. In 1909 he approved the first purchase by U.S. armed forces of an airplane. Big Bill was the first president to bring one of Edison's Victrolas into the White House. He was the first chief executive to throw a baseball to launch the annual season. Under his administration, the U.S. Post Office for the first time offered parcel post service to patrons.

William Howard Taft home [NATIONAL PARK SERVICE PHOTO BY RAY HENDERSON]

But to him the accomplishments during his years as chief executive paled by comparison with the service he rendered as the first and only ex-president to become Chief Justice of the U.S. Supreme Court. Nominated in 1921 by Warren Harding—yet another Buckeye in Washington—he served with distinction until a few weeks before his death.

In death he managed to set still another precedent, becoming the first president to be buried in the National Cemetery at Arlington, Virginia.

Situated at 2038 Auburn Avenue in Cincinnati and administered by the National Park Service, the William Howard Taft National Historic Site is Big Bill's only monument. For information telephone (513) 241-0343.

At nearby 316 Pike Street, the Taft Museum houses a splendid art collection brought together by the half brother of the president and his wife; telephone (513) 241-0343.

Even Major Archibald Butts is commemorated after a fashion in Ohio. A memorial museum in Sidney commemorates the sinking of the Titanic, *in which Taft's personal aide and his wife were victims. For information call (513) 492-7762.*

3

Crete Garfield Conceived of Air Conditioning for Her Stricken War-Hero Husband

"Poor man, his horse was hit at Chickamauga and somehow he didn't get a scratch. Now this . . . "

Lucretia Garfield, whom her husband called Crete, had noticed Charles J. Guiteau skulking about the White House. But until he shot her husband with a .44 British Bulldog, she considered him "queer, but harmless."

Having been married for twenty-three years, the former Lucretia Randolph was a daughter of a co-founder of the Eclectic Institute at Hiram. She and James Garfield became acquainted at Geauga Seminary in Chester. They saw one another frequently when he became a student at the Eclectic Institute and married two years after his graduation from Williams College in Massachusetts.

Soon after their wedding in her father's home, Crete stopped teaching school to devote full time to her lightly bearded, six-foot husband. Born in a Cuyahoga County log cabin that had been built by his father, Garfield was regarded as a "comer," a man going places, despite his leaning toward the ministry while moving toward a career in education.

Relatives and friends glowed when they learned in 1856 that the twenty-five-year-old would soon become president of the Eclectic Institute. He headed the Hiram college only a few months before beginning to study law and winning an election that sent him to the legislature.

State Senator Garfield campaigned for Abraham Lincoln in 1860 and welcomed the prospect of impending strife. The loss of Fort Sumter at Charleston "was the best thing that

Lucretia Garfield, who thought of artificially lowering air temperature. [LIBRARY OF CONGRESS]

could have happened to the Union," he said. "It galvanized public sentiment throughout the North."

The Union defeat at Bull Run prompted the ardent abolitionist to abandon his career in education. In August 1861 he received his commission as a lieutenant colonel, authorized to raise the Forty-second Ohio Regiment. Recruitment went well, but Hiram College was almost emptied to fill the ranks of the regiment.

Once his men learned to stand at attention and to march, Colonel Garfield led them to Louisville. There fellow Buckeye Don Carlos Buell was so impressed with the "soldierly condition" of the Forty-second that he put its leader in charge of a brigade. Assigned the task of driving Confederate General Humphrey Marshall from the state, Garfield moved forward with about 1,100 men—and no artillery.

He faced a rebel force of 5,000, fortified with a dozen cannon. With no military training, Garfield proved an able strategist who moved his men so often that his foes became confused. The opposing forces met at Middle Creek on January 10, 1862. Forgotten in the aftermath of major battles, this early engagement, then crucial, saw badly outnumbered Union forces win the day.

Abraham Lincoln was so impressed that he made Garfield a brigadier general; voters of Ohio then elected him to the U.S. House of Representatives. Instead of taking off his uniform, he fought at Shiloh and at Corinth, then became chief of staff to Ohio's Major General William S. Rosecrans, head of the Army of the Cumberland.

It was in this capacity that he fought at Chickamauga. Serving as a battlefield courier, Garfield rode through heavy fire to take General George H. Thomas word that the Union right was crumbling. Thomas succeeded in holding the left, thus saving the day for Federal forces.

The grateful president rewarded Garfield with a commission as major general, then persuaded him that his services were more badly needed in the capital than on the battlefield.

Garfield reluctantly backed Lincoln's bid for re-election and later voted for the impeachment of Andrew Johnson. During seventeen years in Congress, he won such respect that he became the leader of the Republican minority and was elected to the U.S. Senate by the Ohio legislature.

James A. Garfield never occupied his Senate seat, however.

An assassin's pistol sent two bullets into Garfield's body while he waited in a Washington railroad station. [Harper's Weekly]

On the day he was scheduled to do so, he was inaugurated as president of the United States, having won 4,454,416 popular votes against 4,444,952 for now-forgotten Democrat Winfield Scott Hancock.

It seems to have been Garfield's sudden and unexpected surge to the top that prompted Guiteau to stalk him with a handgun he thought "would look nice in a museum some day." Felled on July 2, 1881, by two bullets fired in the waiting room of the Baltimore and Potomac railroad station in Washington, D.C., Garfield was rushed to the White House. There his wife brushed all objections aside and insisted upon a procedure so radical that it had never been tried.

"We heat our houses in winter," she insisted. "Why on earth can't we cool at least one big room for a man who is fighting for his life?" To aides, she issued a set of hurried orders: "Go out and buy ice—big pieces of it—and plenty of tubs, along with palmetto fans."

Once the Ohio woman's crude system was in place, she, her children, and staff members waved fans to circulate the hot summer air whose temperature had been lowered by melting ice. After the world's first "air conditioning system" went into operation on July 12, it was found that by melting 100 pounds of ice per hour, room temperature could be lowered significantly.

Crete Garfield's ingenuity might have saved the life of her husband, had not unsterilized hands and instruments of surgeons led to blood poisoning. After seventy-nine days of pain, the president died. But he left behind his wife's radical idea, born in frantic action to save a man who had been unharmed by a hail of Confederate bullets at Chickamauga.

Lawnfield, at 8095 Mentor Avenue in Mentor, is the restored thirty-room home of James A. Garfield; telephone (216) 255-8722.

Garfield's tomb and monument are in Lakeview Cemetery, Cleveland. Other notables buried there include John D. Rockefeller and Mark Hanna; telephone (216) 421-2665.

4

Hayes Squeaked Through the Closest Presidential Contest

Rutherford B. Hayes, born in Delaware, Ohio, was the first to go to the White House by only one vote in the electoral college. Barring a third-party candidate far more effective than was Ross Perot in 1992, he probably was also the last to win in this fashion.

Baby Rutherford didn't arrive at the Williams Street home until eleven weeks after his father's death. Dr. Reuben Lamb is said to have collected a fee of $3.50 for his services in delivering the president-to-be.

Sardis Birchard, a brother of his mother, Sophia Hayes, helped her to rear the boy whom he came to regard as his son. At age fourteen Rutherford left the local school to attend an academy at Norwalk. He spent a period at a Connecticut academy, then enrolled at Kenyon College.

As valedictorian of the class of 1842, he found it easy to be admitted to Harvard Law School. Two years later his Uncle Sardis, who had paid his tuition, beamed with pride when his ward was admitted to the Ohio bar sixty days after returning home.

Barely making enough to survive in Sandusky, Hayes moved to Cincinnati in 1850, where he slept in his office to keep his expenses to thirty dollars a month. After two years he had money enough to marry his childhood sweetheart, Lucy Webb. Their uneventful lifestyle came to an end when Confederates fired upon Fort Sumter. Already prominent on the Cincinnati political scene, Hayes pleaded for negotiations and even compromise between the warring sections. When he found this futile, he enlisted in the Twenty-third Ohio

Mrs. Hayes, who was the first First Lady to hold a college degree, frowned on alcohol and was derided as "Lemonade Lucy." [LIBRARY OF CONGRESS]

Regiment of Volunteers as a major under the command of Colonel William S. Rosecrans.

Soon a crisis developed. Having been issued old flintlock muskets, many members of the Twenty-third—including a skinny private named William McKinley—refused to accept them. Major Hayes promised to get modern weapons soon, pointed out that George Washington's troops had fought with muskets, and managed to avert a potential mutiny.

Initially sent to West Virginia to quell activities of bushwhackers, the Twenty-third Ohio served for the duration but saw comparatively little battlefield action. Hayes, who rose to the rank of brevet major general, had four horses shot from under him and never tired of telling how he helped thwart John Hunt Morgan's Ohio raid of 1863.

Hence, it was as a war hero that he was nominated for the U.S. House of Representatives. Refusing to campaign, he won handily but remained in uniform until June 1865. A decade later, after having served two terms as governor, Hayes was persuaded to seek that office once more. To his diary he confided on April 14, 1875, "Several suggest that if elected governor now, I will stand well for the Presidency next year. How wild! What a queer lot we are becoming!"

When Republicans converged upon Cincinnati in 1876 to pick a candidate, James G. Blaine of Maine was the odds-on favorite who quickly came within twenty-seven votes of this goal. On the seventh ballot, however, Blaine's opponents rallied to Hayes and gave him the nomination—by a margin of six votes.

Many politicians said the Buckeye didn't have a chance, even though he said he was unwilling to serve more than four years. Fearing the possibility of a third term for Grant, Congress warned it should not happen; it "would be unwise, unpatriotic, and fraught with peril to our free institutions." Angry about corruption and scandal in the Grant administration, voters everywhere appeared ready to send a Democrat to the White House for the first time in two decades.

The Democrats convened in St. Louis for the first national convention held west of the Mississippi River and nominated Samuel J. Tilden of New York. Pitted against him, Hayes was considered to be the underdog. Tilden had become a national hero as a result of his role in breaking up the notorious Tweed political ring of New York City. That made it easy for his followers to crusade against Grant's record on what they called "a reform ticket." To boost their candidate's chances

A Republican cartoonist claimed to depict Democrats using force to gain votes in the South. [HARPER'S WEEKLY]

Admitting that refusal to concede votes might lead to bloodshed, Tilden's manager said he preferred four years of Hayes to four years of war.
[HARPER'S WEEKLY]

even more, Democrats for the first time in U.S. history employed professional publicity men to manage their campaign.

Republicans responded by putting nonpolitical notables on the campaign trail; even Mark Twain stumped for Hayes. Since reform was in the air, party orators stressed their support for "cleaning up the civil service." Many of them also "waved the bloody shirt," charging that the Democrats had permitted sectional rivalry to reach a state where it could be settled only by war.

On one point both aspirants for the White House agreed: it was time to begin to withdraw all Federal troops from the occupied South. Neither man took to the hustings, for it was then considered undignified for a man to advocate his own election to the nation's highest office.

On election night Hayes and most of his followers accepted what seemed to be inevitable. A Democratic sweep of the South, combined with narrow wins in Connecticut, Delaware, and Indiana, indicated that Samuel J. Tilden would become the nineteenth president. But John C. Reid, managing editor of the *New York Times*, continued to check results after Hayes went to bed. Consulting three comrades, Reid found that they agreed with him that contested results in the

South could well determine the outcome. Florida's four electoral votes were in doubt; so were Louisiana's eight and South Carolina's seven.

A special post-election edition of the *Times* reported that with 185 electoral votes needed for a victory, Tilden had 184 and Hayes had 181. This tally assumed that Louisiana and South Carolina would enter the Hayes column, with Florida still in doubt.

Republican leaders immediately sent special representatives to the South; among them was James A. Garfield, who watched the counting of votes in Louisiana. There, Democrats reported 83,723 votes for Tilden, but Republicans charged that he actually got only 70,508.

Oral tradition insists that "a great deal of Republican money was spent in contested southern states." Whether that was the case or not, returns considered official by party leaders gave Florida, South Carolina, and Louisiana to Hayes. In Oregon, the state's single vote remained in limbo.

Members of the electoral college met in December but soon found themselves unable to act. Each of the three contested southern states sent two teams, one representing Republicans

Tilden, famous as a political reformer, was mocked by cartoonist Thomas Nast. [HARPER'S WEEKLY]

and Hayes, the other claiming victory for Democrats and Tilden. Members of the Republican-controlled U.S. Senate said that the president of their body should conduct the count. Democrats, who had a majority in the House of Representatives, insisted that the votes should be counted by their speaker.

In this dilemma, both bodies of lawmakers backed an Electoral Commission Law. Under its terms, congressional powers were delegated to a special body of fifteen men. When created, the commission included three Republican and two Democratic senators, three Democratic and two Republican representatives, and two Republican and two Democratic justices of the Supreme Court.

The justices were empowered to add an unbiased colleague to their number. They chose David Davis, who had retired from the court to become a senator from Illinois. After having managed Abraham Lincoln's 1860 campaign, Davis now listed himself as a political independent.

He soon resigned from the commission, and Republican justice Joseph Philo Bradley of New Jersey was selected to take his place. Hence the commission now included eight Republicans and seven Democrats.

Often working in the presence of a sixty- to ninety-man

In another "first," Hayes took his oath of office in secret on Sunday night, March 3, 1877, then took it again in public the following day. [LIBRARY OF CONGRESS]

Cartoonist Thomas Nast, who created both the Democratic donkey and the Republican elephant, depicted the latter as wailing, "Another such victory, and I am undone." [HARPER'S WEEKLY]

HERE
LIES
THE
DEMOCRATIC
TIGER
GREATLY WEAKENED
BY THE BEHAVIOR
OF FILIBUSTERS

press corps, commissioners began counting votes on February 1. Days of discussion were devoted to each contested state, but always the outcome was eight to seven. In the early morning hours of March 2, the chairman announced that Rutherford B. Hayes had received 185 votes, a total that included all 20 challenged votes, and would therefore become the next president of the United States.

Though no one questioned that one contested vote would have made him the winner, Tilden did not protest the decision. Later observers have labeled the contest of 1876 as "the stolen election." Tilden did not call it that; he wanted no more strife, insisting that carpetbag government in the South must end.

Washington gossip declared there was a formal swap of the White House for the end of Reconstruction. Whether or not that was the case, the last Federal troops of occupation were soon ordered from the South by the Buckeye who gained the presidency by a single vote.

Spiegel Grove, a twenty-five-acre site at Hayes and Buckland avenues in Fremont where the president and Lucy once lived, is now the Hayes Presidential Center. A memorial building houses family mementos and the public and private papers of the president and his family; telephone (419) 332-2081.

5
Annie Oakley's Guns Brought Her Lasting Fame

In Berlin, Germany, members of the elite Union Club gathered at the Charlottenburg race course on November 13, 1897, to see an Ohio-born woman's private performance that included seventeen shooting events. Annie Oakley began by showing her prowess in rifle shooting of clay pigeons "straight," as her hosts described the activity. She then pulled the trap herself and downed more clay pigeons. Soon she showed how she could snatch the gun from the ground after the trap was sprung and maintain unerring marksmanship. In the fourteenth event she broke six balls that had gone into the air in four seconds. As a finale, she downed twelve live pigeons at twenty-five yards with a 20-gauge shotgun.

Germany's Kaiser Wilhelm I was behind the invitation to give a private performance for the elite of the capital. In an earlier exhibition, Annie had awed a large crowd by shooting ash from a cigarette in the lips of his grandson. The twenty-eight-year-old prince who took part in her act later achieved worldwide notoriety during World War I as Kaiser Wilhelm II.

Like James Garfield, Phoebe Anne Oakley Mozee (or Moses) was born in one of many log cabins in Darke County. In 1860 much of Ohio was still pioneer country, and log cabins abounded.

Her father's death when she was four years old left the girl, her mother, and her seven siblings in dire poverty. Matters became so bad that at age nine Annie began to shoot rabbits and quail for the family table. Folk who remembered her childhood insisted that no one taught her how to handle a gun. "From the start, she was a dead shot," they testified in later years.

Since her parents were Quakers, to some outsiders it seemed strange that they kept a gun. But among many Friends, a weapon was listed as a tool necessary for survival on the frontier. That's how in 1855 Jacob Moses was able to take along a cap-and-ball rifle when he and his brood moved from Pennsylvania to a tiny rented farm in Ohio.

It was her father's old muzzleloader that Annie used to furnish the family with meat. The gun was considerably taller than the girl when she first pulled it to the floor of their cabin, and it soon began adding squirrels and pheasants to their larder.

By this time Annie's mother, Suzanne, had lost a second husband and had taken a third. Although Joe Shaw loved his wife's children, he couldn't provide for them. He was barely able to meet payments on the $200 a year family mortgage. Writer Courtney Riley Cooper later pointed out that few mortgages were then renewed. A person forked over cash at

Center stage, waiting for a target [AUTHOR'S COLLECTION]

Artist's interpretation of the Ohio woman on horseback. [AUTHOR'S COLLECTION]

every payment period, or lost everything. That, said Cooper, made the mortgage "the ogre of rural America."

By the time Annie was thirteen, she knew the meaning of the mortgage on the farm purchased when she was very young. Aware of her stepfather's financial difficulties, she discovered that quail and other game were wanted by fancy folk in Cincinnati and Dayton.

In nearby Greenville, Anthony and Charles Katzenberger had earlier made an occasional purchase from "the girl who made most other hunters look clumsy." Now they arranged to ship small game to cities by stagecoach, functioning as middlemen for Annie's increasingly larger sales.

According to her autobiography, as soon as she struck a deal with the Katzenbergers, she "donned a linsey dress" and headed for the woods. That day, she became the world's first female to make her living by the skilled use of guns. By the time she was sixteen, Annie had taken over the installment payments on the mortgage. As a special reward for their protégé, the Katzenbergers gave her a sack of percussion caps, five pounds of shot, and one pound of DuPont black powder.

It was the first high-grade powder she had ever used, and her skill attracted so much admiration that neighbors bought her a 16-gauge breechloader and six or eight dozen brass shells. So equipped, she began to ship pelts and game to the Katzenbergers in lots of one dozen. Before her mother's mortgage was retired, she had made such a reputation at turkey shoots that she was no longer allowed to enter them.

Word of the exploits of the tiny female spread throughout the region. Jack Frost, one of the first Cincinnati hotel keepers to buy her game, saw an opportunity to capitalize on her talents. Three noted marksmen headed by Frank Butler were appearing at a nearby theater. It was customary to arrange a match, complete with side bets, between visitors and some local marksman. Frost made the arrangements without identifying the local opponent, placed a bet of $100, and then sent for fifteen-year-old Annie Moses.

Frank Butler and his diminutive opponent were tied after each had brought down twenty-four trap-released birds. Butler missed his next shot, but Annie did not and won the

Buffalo Bill's Deadwood Coach, in London, England (William F. Cody standing). [OHIO STATE HISTORICAL SOCIETY

first match of this sort in which she participated. Jack Frost collected his winnings on the spot, and seven years later Annie became Mrs. Frank Butler.

Using Annie Oakley as her stage name, she and Frank joined the four-ring circus organized by the Sells brothers of Dublin, Ohio. That put them in competition with a "coal black sacred elephant," acting dogs Jack and George, and a trained bear called Jenny.

Butler, who later gave up performing to become his wife's manager, learned that a noted Native American was in St. Paul, Minnesota, when their circus arrived in town. Somehow, he arranged for Annie to meet Sitting Bull and to demonstrate her skill for him. Legend says that the great warrior spontaneously dubbed Annie as *Watanya cicilia*, a title which, translated, stuck to "Little Sure Shot" for the rest of her life.

When Sells Brothers Circus and Buffalo Bill's Wild West Show were playing in New Orleans simultaneously, it was natural for Frank and Annie to become acquainted with Colonel William F. Cody. Intrigued by the woman already hailed as the best shot in the Western world, Cody took her into his highly publicized show.

Annie occasionally wore feathers, perhaps in memory of Sitting Bull. [AUTHOR'S COLLECTION]

Annie about the time she and Frank joined Sells Brothers Circus. [AUTHOR'S COLLECTION]

During seventeen years with Buffalo Bill, Annie performed before notables in America and Europe. Queen Victoria and her prime minister, William E. Gladstone, came to see the Ohio woman shoot; so did the royal heads of Germany, Sweden, Greece, Belgium, and Denmark.

For the entertainment of common folk as well as royalty, Annie Oakley hit thousands of glass balls and dimes tossed into the air. During a record day, she brought down 4,772 out of 5,000. Using a mirror, she shot with her back turned to her target, frequently clipping cigarettes from the lips of her husband.

One of her most memorable feats consisted of slicing from thirty paces an ordinary playing card held with thin edge toward her. As a variant, she would drill four or five holes in a card as it fluttered to the ground. So many playing cards were punched by Annie's bullets that a theatrical pass or a complimentary ticket is still commonly known as an "Annie Oakley."

After her death in 1926, Little Sure Shot became even more famous than during her decades as a performer. Barbara Stanwyck played the title role in the 1935 movie *Annie Oakley.* Five years later, Rodgers and Hammerstein produced on Broadway the musical *Annie Get Your Gun*, directed by Joshua Logan. More than any other actress who played the role, it was Ethel Merman who made Annie Oakley immortal on the stage during the musical's three-year run. Metro-Goldwyn-Mayer put Betty Hutton into the title role in its 1950 film version of the musical. Seven years later, Mary Martin played Annie for television audiences.

Most of these Annies wouldn't have known a .22 rim fire from a hammerless 12-gauge shotgun, the all-time favorite weapon of the Ohio woman.

Numerous Annie Oakley prizes and mementos are on display at the Garst Museum, 205 North Broadway Street, Greenville; telephone (513) 548-5250. Annually, this city is the site of the Annie Oakley Festival, held during the last full weekend of July.

6

Literally, Not Figuratively, Vallandigham Became a Man Without a Country

"What on earth are you doing to my house?"

"Coming in!" responded an ax-wielding member of the 115th Ohio Regiment. "You may as well give yourself up!"

"Never!" shouted gubernatorial candidate Clement L. Vallandigham from the second floor of his Dayton home. "I have committed no crime."

"General Burnside says otherwise. Come on down, now, and don't give us any more trouble!"

That pre-dawn exchange on May 6, 1863, led to the arrest of a former U.S. congressman, previously the editor and co-owner of the Dayton *Empire* newspaper.

Possibly because Ohio was thought to be a haven for a poisonous snake, Vallandigham and other "Peace Democrats" were widely called Copperheads. Especially numerous among the Irish who opposed conscription for military service, Copperheads everywhere regarded the Buckeye editor as their leader.

A native of New Lisbon, at age twenty-five Vallandigham became the youngest member of the Ohio legislature. Sent to the U.S. House of Representatives in 1858, he became noted as a critic of policies likely to lead to war.

Abraham Lincoln's election to the presidency put the two men on a collision course. Refusing to support war measures taken by Lincoln without congressional authorization, the man from New Lisbon minced no words. "The usurpation of Lincoln in daring to raise and support armies by executive proclamation," he said in May 1861, "deserves impeachment."

Armed with rifles and axes, members of the 115th Ohio regiment arrested Vallandigham at his Dayton residence. [*FRANK LESLIE'S ILLUSTRATED WEEKLY*]

Against the wishes of Lincoln and of Congress, he urged that Jewish rabbis be admitted to the U.S. Army as chaplains. He voted against conscription and called revocation of the writ of *habeas corpus* dictatorial. Lincoln, he said, had made the North "an imperial despotism."

That is why political rivals cut supporters from his district by means of a gerrymander. Ousted from his congressional seat, he announced his candidacy for the governorship and seemed headed for victory until Ambrose Burnside was put in charge of the military Department of the Ohio.

Three weeks after assuming his new role, Burnside issued General Order No. 38. In it he warned that "all persons found within our lines, who commit acts for the benefit of the enemies of our country, will be tried as spies or traitors, and, if convicted, will suffer death."

A person did not have to write secret letters or recruit for the Confederacy to be labeled a traitor. All it took was "the habit of declaring sympathy for the enemy." Those who did that, said Burnside, would be tried as traitors or sent from Union territory.

Candidate Vallandigham spoke to an audience of about

20,000 at Mount Vernon on May 4. He remained calm until he pulled from his pocket a copy of Order No. 38. Ignoring an army captain who was taking notes, the Copperhead cried that he despised the document. When the crowd roared approval, he shouted that he "spit upon it and trampled it under his feet."

Arrested in the pre-dawn hours of May 6, Vallandigham was jailed in Cincinnati. Eight military officers deliberated only three hours before finding him guilty of "expressing treasonable sympathy for the enemy." Burnside then ordered him sent to Fort Warren in Boston harbor, to be held in close confinement.

There the matter would have ended had not public indignation throughout the North created a crisis in Washington. Governor Horatio Seymour of New York called the conviction "an act which has brought dishonor upon our country." Burnside offered his resignation, which elicited from Lincoln a terse note indicating that every member of the cabinet regretted the arrest.

Vallandigham (at extreme left) *and fellow Copperheads were derided as not welcome in Richmond.* [*HARPER'S WEEKLY*]

Handsome and articulate, Vallandigham made life miserable for Abraham Lincoln. [BRADY STUDIO, LIBRARY OF CONGRESS]

Scores of protests that reached the White House were ignored; Lincoln penned one lengthy explanation in which he argued: "Must I shoot a simple-minded soldier boy who deserts, while I must not touch a hair of the wily agitator who induces him to desert?"

Presidential secretaries John Nicolay and John Hay, authors of the first comprehensive biography of Lincoln, devoted thirty-two pages to the Vallandigham affair. Lincoln was delighted, they told readers, when he found that there was an escape clause in the Burnside order.

Almost as an afterthought to threats of execution, the general had offered an alternative: "deportation beyond our lines to the lines of their friends." Seizing upon this clause, Lincoln ordered Vallandigham from U.S. soil and sent him to Buckeye General William Rosecrans in Tennessee for delivery to the Confederate States of America. The first and only ex-congressman to be exiled, Vallandigham was not welcomed in Richmond. Soon he made his way to Wilmington, North Carolina, then to Canada by way of Bermuda.

Intensely moved by the experiences of a man he had never met, Edward Everett Hale used the banishment of the Buckeye lawmaker as the basis for his famous short story, "The Man Without a Country."

PART TWO

Trailblazers and Pioneers

Partly, perhaps, because for years Ohio represented the growing edge of the nation as it gradually expanded westward, the roll of its trailblazers and pioneers is long.

Anthony Wayne helped the British to understand the meaning of "colonial resistance" at Fort Defiance. During the Civil War, Clara Barton won international renown. But it was Mary Anne Ball Bickerdyke of Knox City who became "Mother" to countless Federal soldiers. Alone among pioneer female nurses, she boldly went to the West and at Cairo, Illinois, showed that a military hospital can be clean. Horace Mann blazed trails in education, and Clarence Darrow effected lasting changes in our concept of justice.

For decades, the Erie Canal symbolized America's passion for doing the impossible. Buckeyes whose personal stories are included here did just that. Had experts at the time surveyed their backgrounds and opportunities, they would have scoffed at the notion any of them would have had wide and lasting impact.

Moses Cleaveland looked every inch the leader when portrayed in John H. Kennedy's History of the City of Cleveland *(1896).*

7

Moses Cleaveland Found
"The American Promised Land"

"You white people, all you want is here!" Patting the pocket in which he kept a few coins, Red Jacket stooped low so he could look upward at the settler who had come to bargain for land claimed by the Iroquois.

"You think you are high above warriors of the Six Nations. You say you come to live among them as brothers and show them how to make their fields rich."

"No, no," interrupted Moses Cleaveland. "We only want peace in which to work the land."

"You bring tools and tell good stories," admitted the chieftain who had been given a red jacket by the British who came to subdue rebellious colonists. "Sagoyewatha knows the truth. You will farm our land, then drive us away."

According to John Holley, a member of Cleaveland's party, the dialogue took place after two days of feasting and drinking at Skinner's Tavern in Buffalo, New York, on June 23, 1796. Red Jacket, who spoke through an interpreter, was ready to trade but didn't want to admit it.

Three hours of haggling led to terms. Some white men who were present later bragged that they got the Indians' title to about 3,300,000 acres for one hundred gallons of whiskey and two beef cattle. James A. Garfield, who later investigated the story with great care, insisted that before accepting the commodities Red Jacket and his warriors pocketed five hundred English pounds.

Cleaveland and his colleagues had already paid the state of Connecticut about forty cents per acre for the land in ques-

A vast region between the Mississippi and Ohio rivers formed the Northwest Territory. [HARPER'S ENCYCLOPEDIA OF U.S. HISTORY (1905)]

tion. However, to attract settlers, it was vital to make terms with its Indian claimants. So when the survey party led by Cleaveland reached Canandaigua, New York, there was a second parley. This time, the Indian leader was Thayendanegea, known to white men as Joseph Brant.

Notorious throughout the frontier, Brant and Red Jacket had fought with the British during the American Revolution. Less than twenty years before meeting the settlers bound for what they called the Western Reserve, Brant had led an attack upon a settlement in what is now Otsego County, New York. When eight hundred Redcoats and warriors descended upon Cherry Valley, its sixteen soldiers were quickly subdued. All the soldiers and half of the settlers were killed, with the rest taken into captivity.

Mellowed by passing years and no longer actively at war with the former colonists, Thayendanegea smoked the peace pipe with Cleaveland. "Do you remember the battle of Fallen Timbers?" the man from Connecticut prodded. Receiving a series of vigorous nods, he continued: "When peace was made by General Anthony Wayne at Greenville, Indian land came to the white man. But since no Mohawk chieftain signed, we will pay you well to let us pass in peace."

Tradition says that forty-four-year-old Cleaveland again parted with money, whiskey, and cattle. In return, he and his party were promised that they could travel to faraway Lake Erie.

They represented the nation's first formally established company of land developers, probably formed as a result of Cleaveland's knowledge of the law. A 1777 graduate of Yale College, he had served with George Washington at Valley Forge before winning a seat in the state legislature while still in the uniform of the Connecticut State Militia.

Made a general in 1796, Cleaveland pored over statutes and records of land transactions until he found what he called "the American Promised Land." Under Connecticut's royal charter, land claimed by the colony originally stretched westward across the continent. During the organization of former colonies into states, much of it had been ceded to the new national government. However, many days' journey to the west, a tract south of Lake Erie had been retained. Lawmakers hoped to repay victims of the British by making free land available to them in "Fire Lands" within the state's Western Reserve.

Having inside information about Connecticut's growing financial problems, Moses Cleaveland put up about $32,000 of his own money to organize the Connecticut Land Company. Eventually including nearly sixty persons, this pioneer syndicate agreed on September 2, 1795, to pay $1.2 million for all of the Western Reserve outside the Fire Lands.

Investors hoped to make big profits; if they could dispose of their portion of the Western Reserve at $1.25 an acre, they would triple their money. However, for this to happen, the land must be surveyed and laid out in townships. Cleaveland, who was one of seven company directors, persuaded his colleagues to make him their general agent. In this capacity, he recruited a party of more than forty assistants and prepared to go to "the Promised Land."

They assembled at Schenectady early in the spring of 1796 and went up the Mohawk River in bateaux. From Little Falls, according to Garfield, they took their tiny vessels overland to Wood Creek. Moving downstream, they came to Oneida Lake, then went down the Oswego River to Lake Ontario and Niagara. From that point it was a comparatively short journey to Lake Erie. En route, Cleaveland doled out trifling sums to Red Jacket and Joseph Brant.

Seth Pease, a member of the survey party who kept a diary, recorded that some of them reached New Connecticut on July 4 "and gave three cheers precisely at five o'clock P.M." Cleaveland insisted that the spot on what he called Conneaugh Creek be named Fort Independence. Once that matter was settled, his followers fired a "federal salute of 15 rounds," followed by a final round in honor of New Connecticut.

On July 22 the party jubilantly reached the mouth of the Cuyahoga River, where they planned to establish their capital city. Cleaveland personally paced out a public square he estimated to be ten acres in size, then he put his surveyors to work plotting a town around it. His men insisted upon naming the not-yet-built town in his honor, but he remained in the region only until October. Back in Connecticut, he resumed his profitable law practice and never returned to the American Promised Land to which an English-speaking Moses had led the way. There is no record that he recovered his initial investment.

Some investors paid their share of the purchase price in the form of promissory notes, which Connecticut had trouble collecting. Though townships were named and laid out, settlers were afraid to make the long and dangerous journey from the East. As a result, land did not sell except at rock-bottom prices, usually accompanied by the gift of a tract to establish a gristmill.

Cleaveland and Sandusky were home to the first two families who settled permanently in the Reserve. By 1799 it held an estimated thirty-two small settlements but still had no effective form of government.

Another blow came in 1800. The purchase of the Northwest Territory by the United States had raised the question of who governed New Connecticut. After investigation, a congressional committee headed by John Marshall ruled that the region was not subject to the authority of the territory and that Connecticut was too far away to exercise jurisdiction. In this dilemma, national lawmakers passed and President John Adams signed the "Quieting Act," designed to end squabbling in the region. Under its terms Arthur St. Clair, head of the Northwest Territory, took charge. Soon he put the entire Western Reserve into a single county, Trumbull, and designated Warren as the seat of its government.

By 1811, the American Promised Land had been divided into four additional counties: Geauga, Portage, Cuyahoga, and Ashtabula. Many Indians remained within the region until the outbreak of the War of 1812, during which most sided with the British.

Moses Cleaveland and his band of pioneers proved right in one important respect. The site they chose for the capital city of their land development had an ideal location and began to

John Marshall, destined later to head the U.S. Supreme Court, informed settlers that they were in a legal no-man's land. [NATIONAL ARCHIVES]

Eager to put quarrels over land titles to an end, President John Adams signed the "Quieting Act" without hesitation.
[NATIONAL ARCHIVES]

attract settlers as soon as the War of 1812 came to a close. Completion of New York's Erie Canal made it a boom town to which enterprising adventurers succeeded in transporting a printing press and quantities of type with which they launched the *Cleaveland Gazette & Commercial Register* newspaper.

Tradition has it that when attempting to prepare a new masthead for the paper, typesetters used letters so large that the title overran the edge of the paper. Unwilling to be stopped by so trifling a matter, the printers dropped the letter *A* from the masthead, and Cleveland was so named.

Never the capital of what is now Ohio, Cleveland soon emerged as a major industrial and financial center of the surrounding region. Yet when its elegant courthouse was completed and dedicated, no one present dreamed that a fifty-two-story skyscraper would eventually stand nearby. Neither did anyone envision that the city would nurture the man destined to become the world's first billionaire—John D. Rockefeller.

For detailed information about Cleveland's many historic sites and visitor attractions, contact the chamber of commerce at (216) 975-3100.

8

"That Road Will Make Ohio the Breadbasket of the Nation!"

Jeremiah Morrow signaled for silence.

"I know you are enjoying your conversations; some of you seldom see one another. But we have important business— top secret—to conduct," the governor of Ohio began.

"You didn't say anything about secrecy in your letter of invitation," objected Simon Perkins of Akron. "I prefer to conduct my business entirely above the board."

"This is different," Morrow explained. "It's about the road. All of us know we're helpless without action in Washington."

As heads nodded solemnly, the presiding officer continued: "I shall try to be brief. We are especially honored to have General Harrison present. Senator Ruggles will refresh the memories of those who are not entirely familiar with our opportunity—and our dilemma."

Pointing toward a portrait of the state's first governor, Ruggles began, "Congress first acted when Edward Tiffin and the rest of our government were at Chillicothe. A congressional act of March 1806 authorized President Jefferson to name commissioners."

"He wasted no time," interrupted former governor Ethan Allen Brown. "And as soon as they were named, they began looking at Zane's Trace."

"That was logical; Ebenezer Zane had done his work a full ten years earlier. Most of you remember that he crossed the Ohio at Wheeling, then worked his way westward to Chillicothe by way of Zanesville and Lancaster."

"Where did he stop?" a member of the informal planning group inquired.

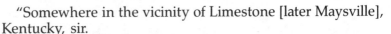

*Gen. William Henry
Harrison won the presidency
as a result of victory in the
battle of Tippecanoe.*
[LIBRARY OF CONGRESS]

"Somewhere in the vicinity of Limestone [later Maysville], Kentucky, sir.

"I regret to say that Zane was less interested in the course of his bridle path than in the three sections of land he received for making the trace. But once laid out, its course has changed but little through the years.

"No need to shake your heads in wonder," Ruggles continued. "That route is likely to be in use when all of us are gone. We're here to try to undo some of the damage done by President Monroe."

"When Monroe vetoed a bill authorizing the federal government to collect tolls, that sounded like the end; I was in the Senate at the time," observed Brown.

"Here in Ohio, we did our best; I hope the road will reach Columbus within a year or two. But we are still struggling with the cost of moving the seat of our government to this site. Unless we get federal dollars, the road will never be finished," Morrow interjected.

"You are here at my invitation, with the hope that you will pull strings in Washington."

William Henry Harrison, wearing the uniform in which he had won national fame, spoke up for the first time. "Completion of the National Road will make Ohio the breadbasket of the nation," he predicted, "and maybe the marketplace, too."

Having heartily endorsed a determined effort to achieve that goal, Ohio leaders returned to their homes scattered throughout the state.

Because it started at Cumberland, Maryland, on the Potomac River, the lengthy trail was officially known as the Cumberland Road. But especially in Ohio, ordinary folk spoke of it simply as "the National." On sections that had been completed, it was not unusual for an east-bound traveler to encounter a west-bound team every three or four miles. Boosters rejoiced in 1825 when William Henry Harrison went to the U.S. Senate with a promise to "bend heaven and earth on behalf of the National."

However, it was not until 1833, during the presidency of Andrew Jackson, that the road reached Columbus. Five years later, Congress made yet another appropriation that was designed to take the Cumberland Road toward Vandalia, Illinois, then capital of the westernmost state.

A fiscal conservative where public projects were involved, James Monroe vetoed the proposal to erect toll booths along the Cumberland Road to help pay for its completion. [LIBRARY OF CONGRESS (REMBRANT PEALE PORTRAIT)]

Had he not died just one month after going to the White House, William Henry Harrison would have pushed for rapid completion. His successors, John Tyler and James K. Polk, had little interest in the biggest public works program undertaken by the United States up to that time. Hence it was a decade after Harrison's death before a state corporation completed the road through Indiana. By that time its importance had diminished because of the impact of railroads and canals.

Still, the handiwork of Ebenezer Zane could be clearly seen upon the map; the macadamized National Road, launched with a congressional appropriation of $30,000, followed Zane's Trace precisely. Years later the route became U.S. Highway 40, a pioneer stretch for use by drivers of automobiles instead of ox wagons. Today Interstate Highway 70 rolls from Martins Ferry to the Indiana state line very close to

Himself the owner of vast tracts of western land, Thomas Jefferson applauded the idea of building a road designed to link the Potomac and Ohio rivers. [LIBRARY OF CONGRESS]

the bridle path traced by Zane before the turn of the nineteenth century.

With its construction stretched out for nearly twenty years
after Governor Morrow had urged its completion, the cost of
the National Road, which had been launched with a pittance,
reached a total of $6,821,246—the largest sum expended up
to that time on any highway. While that total was being
reached, the road achieved another record, of sorts. It was
the subject of sixty separate acts of Congress during half a
century and the administrations of eleven U.S. presidents.

Many who were present for Morrow's "council of war" in
Columbus were dead by the time the ribbon of macadam
stretched all the way across the state. Tradition has it that one
survivor of the history-making session remembered Harrison's assessment and rejoiced:

"Now that the National is finally finished, it has given us a
new name. One of our great cities is now the pork processing
center of the world. As a result, many outsiders make fun of
Cincinnati by calling it Porkopolis. In my book, that's a real
good name for an above-ground gold mine!"

*At Zanesville, a museum situated on U.S. Highway 40, just east
of exit 164 on Interstate 70, traces development of the National Road
from Cumberland, Maryland, to Vandalia, Illinois. Closed December through February; telephone number (614) 454-6851.*

9
Betsy Zane Insisted That No One Would Cry for Her

"We're nearly out of powder; they'll take us soon, if we don't get more!"

"Your brother Ebenezer has plenty in the blockhouse," protested a member of the tiny party defending Fort Henry.

"True. But it's forty yards from here, and the sun is still high. The Indians and Tories will see anyone who tries to make it through the clearing. It will take a brave volunteer to risk his life."

"I'll go!" exclaimed a young man. "If we run out of powder, all sixteen of us will be scalped before night."

"You have a bad leg," objected a comrade. "Stay here and do the best you can to cover me; I can run swiftly."

In the hushed silence that followed, the leader of the defenders, Silas Zane, stared in bewilderment. How could he possibly choose between two men who were willing to try to save the fort even if it should cost one of them his life?"

"You two stay here," Betsy Zane interrupted. "You're needed to fire the muskets. I'll go for powder. If I'm killed, I won't be missed like a man; besides, there's no one to cry for me!"

Probably about fourteen years of age and keenly conscious that many of her female contemporaries were married, Elizabeth Zane is believed to have had no suitor prior to mid-September 1782. That's when a party of the Queen's Rangers, made up of Indians and Tories led by the notorious renegade Simon Girty, headed toward Wheeling in the northwestern neck of Virginia (now West Virginia). On the way, they stopped to take and destroy Fort Henry, almost directly across the Ohio River from their target.

In 1782 the clearing in which Fort Henry stood held only one other structure, the log home of Ebenezer Zane, whose extensive land holdings included much of Wheeling and most of present-day Zanesville farther west on the Muskingum River.

A colonel in the Virginia militia who served as disbursing officer for Lord Dunmore, Ebenezer had anticipated trouble and had secured from the government of Virginia a substantial quantity of gunpowder. Since the fort he had built was unmanned at the time the powder arrived, Zane stored it in his blockhouse.

When news that enemy redcoats and their Native American allies had been seen reached settlers in cabins scattered throughout the forest, they raced into the fort. However, Ebenezer and some members of his family remained in their sturdy blockhouse, which was equipped with loopholes for muskets. Although menfolk in the small company gathered in the tiny fort had brought along their guns and powder horns, they soon were in desperate need of more powder, which was with Zane, a short distance away. That's when the girl known to relatives and friends as Betsy insisted on risking her life.

Most early accounts say that Silas Zane's frantic signals were soon understood by his brother, who unbarred his door, and small Betsy dashed out. Nearby Indians made no attempt to shoot her; some of them simply cried out, "Squaw! Squaw!"

Once she was safely inside her brother's cabin, panting, Ebenezer gestured for Betsy to stand beside the kitchen table. He hastily poured a keg of gunpowder upon the table-cloth, then tied its ends together and fastened the heavy bundle to his little sister's waist.

The weight of the gunpowder made it impossible for Betsy to run as she headed back toward the fort. Watching enemies saw her stumbling attempts to trot, so they opened fire. Bullets whizzed around her and at least two hit the tablecloth. She was leaving trails of gunpowder behind as she reached the door of Fort Henry, uninjured.

When the powder horns of the defenders had been re-filled, there was still a substantial residue. "Load the cannon! Quickly!" Silas Zane commanded.

Using the last of the powder brought to the fort by Betsy, a small cannon was loaded and primed. When its echo boomed through the woods, the startled attackers—who didn't know that it could be fired only once—abandoned what is often described as the last battle of the American Revolution.

Betsy's remarkable exploit attracted wide attention and was described in print very early. In addition to accounts in the *Southern Literary Messenger* and the *Western Messenger,* a detailed story was included in Alexander S. Withers's 1831 volume of *Chronicles of Border Warfare.*

Decades later, a descendant of one person who helped to defend Fort Henry insisted that the teenager who volunteered to go for powder was named Molly Scott. That account is challenged by half a dozen sets of recollections and depositions insisting that Betsy Zane was, indeed, the youngest heroine of the Revolution.

The remains of the young heroine lie in Walnut Grove Cemetery in Martins Ferry. The cemetery is across the Ohio River from Wheeling, West Virginia, where Fort Henry once occupied the site of the city's main street.

To previously circulated accounts, Betsy's youngest son added significant details. According to him, the girl who saved the fort was busy long before the men realized that they were running low on powder.

"Along with her brother Jonathan and a man named Salter, my mother occupied the sentry box," he said she told him many times. "Of course this spot was a target for the enemy, and my mother said she would frequently have to stop and pick out splinters that hit her when bullets split them from protective logs. To a fourteen-year-old, musket balls probably didn't seem much worse than the hail of splinters!"

The Betsy Zane Memorial, erected in honor of her heroism in the defense of Fort Henry, stands at the entrance to Walnut Grove Cemetery in Martins Ferry.

10

Above All, William H. McGuffey Wanted Boys and Girls to Learn

"O, what a sad sight is this! A boy with a dunce cap on his head!" Dipping his quill pen into his inkwell, a Miami University professor continued to write:

"Why does he stand there in front of the school? What has he done?

"He is a bad boy. He talks and laughs in school. He loves to be i-dle, and does not learn his les-son."

These lines may have been written for use with William H. McGuffey's own children and other youngsters who made up his informal back yard school. Or they could have been produced to meet a request of the fledgling publishers Truman and Smith of Cincinnati. Regardless of when and why they were framed, short paragraphs containing few words of more than one syllable and imparting a moral lesson were typical of the most successful first reader ever produced in the United States.

Early biographers thought that McGuffey, born in Pennsylvania, moved to the Ohio frontier as a toddler. However, recent evidence suggests that he was a native Buckeye, probably born in September 1800, within walking distance of Youngstown, a pioneer village of New Connecticut. Whatever the case, the red-haired boy was strongly influenced by the fact that his mother was skilled in reading and writing at a time when most who lived in the untamed Northwest could barely scrawl their names.

Before age six, small William was enrolled in the subscription school of the Reverend William Wick. Soon he became locally renowned for his phenomenal memory; some said

No clear photograph of McGuffey is known to exist. [DICTIONARY OF AMERICAN PORTRAITS, COURTESY OHIO UNIVERSITY]

that he could recite entire books of the Bible without stumbling. While that may be an exaggeration, it prompted believers in phrenology (the "science" of interpreting bumps and shapes of the head) to marvel at "the fullness of his forehead."

His willingness to work, rather than the shape of his forehead, caused Wick to give special heed to him. Though constantly busy with farm chores, the boy found time to pore for hours over his books. He became so proficient that Wick awarded a certificate to him—and suggested that he open a school of his own.

That's how a boy of fourteen came to post notices that on September 1, 1814, he would offer a four-month session of school in the town of Union (later Calcutta). More than forty students, bringing their own books, showed up for instruction that lasted up to ten hours a day, six days a week.

Tradition says that during a subsequent school term of about fifteen weeks, the adolescent teacher was discovered by the Reverend Thomas Hughes. Living about thirty miles away in Darlington, Pennsylvania, Hughes operated the Old Stone Academy and was short of pupils. He invited McGuffey to study with him, and, when the boy hesitated, offered to let him earn tuition of three dollars a year by working as caretaker of the church he served.

When he appeared at the academy, penniless, Hughes put him to work performing household chores so he could earn seventy-five cents a week with which to pay for his "bed and board." During four years in which he learned considerable Latin and a little arithmetic, the boy from Ohio decided he wanted to spend his life as a teacher.

That meant he'd have to go to college, working his way through. Washington College, not far from the Old Stone Academy, accepted him as a student but had no work for him. Consequently, for six years he divided his time between study, teaching, and farm work. Often unable to buy a textbook he needed, he would ask for "one night's loan" and memorize it before dawn.

Finding farm work scarce during the winter of 1826 and still one term short of completing his studies at Washington College, McGuffey decided to open a school of his own. He got the loan of a smokehouse in Paris, Kentucky, and attracted so many pupils that some had to sit outside the building. When the renown of "the boy teacher" reached the

Early dormitories of Miami University were built in 1825. [MIAMI UNIVERSITY]

president of Miami University, he attended a full day of McGuffey's classes and then offered him a job as professor of ancient languages. Soon after he reached Oxford with a packhorse loaded with books and his ten-year-old brother, trustees of the university named him "professor of languages."

Within a few months after settling in Oxford, Professor McGuffey began teaching children who gathered every afternoon in his back yard. Probably influenced by the ideas of Horace Mann, he arranged boys and girls into age groups, giving them reading lessons that varied from week to week. At least as early as 1833 he was satisfied that he had gathered from the Bible, *The New England Primer,* and his own writings enough material to form a textbook for beginning readers.

No one knows whether he went to Truman and Smith in Cincinnati or was approached by them when they heard of his experiments in teaching reading. Nevertheless, wearing knee breeches that had long ago gone out of style, he went to their office to sign a contract.

His *First Reader* and *Second Reader* came from the press in 1836; the third and fourth readers followed a year later. Within a decade an *Eclectic Spelling Book* was prepared by his younger brother, Alexander, and the *Fifth Reader* was published. A primer was issued in 1849, but it was not until 1857 that the series of McGuffey textbooks was completed with the appearance of the *Sixth Reader.*

Comparatively little time and effort seems to have gone into preparation of the books later widely known simply as "McGuffey's." Although his assignment at Miami University required a full work week when students were on the campus, the fledgling author managed to travel often to Columbus where he successfully lobbied legislators to back better training for teachers. A founder of Cincinnati's Western Literary Institute and its president for a term, he persuaded colleagues to support better education for women at a time when this was a highly controversial issue.

Revered by many as a founding father of Ohio's present-day public school system, McGuffey spent his most prolific decade at Miami University. Later he taught at Cincinnati

Many stories and the illustrations that accompany them deal with obedient children who are eager to learn. [AUTHOR'S COLLECTION]

College, Woodward College, and Ohio University before going to the University of Virginia for a twenty-eight-year stint.

Often heavily edited, his little books went through many editions before his death in 1873. By 1920, an estimated 120,000,000 copies of them had been used by successive generations of children in more than half the states of the Union.

In 1928, Henry Ford paid for a reprint of the six McGuffey readers, edition of 1857. A decade earlier, a McGuffey Society to honor and preserve his story had been launched in Columbus. Similar organizations sprang up throughout Ohio, in Jackson, Uhrichsville, Gahauna, and other towns. Indianapolis joined the band in 1925, and New York City followed.

Interest then waned for several decades until the increase in the number of private schools and parental eagerness for stress upon moral values brought McGuffey's readers to the forefront once more. Today, hundreds of school systems are

A revolving eight-sided worktable is a prominent feature of the McGuffey Museum at Miami University. [MIAMI UNIVERSITY]

using one or more of the revised volumes originally written on foolscap by the light of oil-burning lamps.

When new acquaintances congratulated William H. Mc-Guffey on having become rich as a result of his books, he smiled and said nothing. Only his intimates knew that the first four readers brought him a detailed contract on April 28, 1836. Under its terms, the publishers agreed to pay him a royalty of 10 percent on sales of the books priced at 7¢, 12½¢, and 25¢ until the total reached $1,000. After that, McGuffeys were wholly owned by the publishers.

Scholars have generally paid little attention to the man who through his books influenced more students than any other American. Some editions of *The World Book* give almost half a page to the career and influence of McGuffey, but a thirty-volume edition of *The Encyclopedia Americana* deals with him in eighteen lines.

"Bessie Dug Flowers Until the Bell Rang" illustrates one of McGuffey's original stories. [AUTHOR'S COLLECTION]

Money he didn't garner and fame he failed to find in academic circles wouldn't concern the zealous teacher, were he alive today. But he would rejoice that only the Bible and *Webster's Dictionary* are believed to have been so widely influential as his little readers. With his memory once more revived and his books again used throughout the nation, multitudes of teachers and parents revere him as "schoolmaster to the nation." For him, that would be reward enough for all his labors.

Miami University maintains an on-campus McGuffey Museum that is open to tour groups; for information call (513) 529-2232.

11

John H. Patterson Merged Advertising, Sales, and Manufacturing

"This is gorgeous country, but too steep to suit me."

"It's fine for a vacation, but I'm not sure I would want to live here."

"Me either," responded a fellow guest of the Antlers in Colorado Springs. Turning to warm himself before the log fire, he stretched out his hand. "I'm John H. Patterson, of Dayton, Ohio."

"Glad to meet you. I hail from Braintree, Massachusetts, and friends call me Peter Simpson. What are you doing so far from home?"

"My brother, Frank, and I came out to look at ranch land. We've about made up our minds to go into cattle."

"No animals for me. I wouldn't touch a business I couldn't leave behind without worrying about it."

Suddenly intensely interested, Patterson responded, "Frank and I were in coal, but we sold out and have to find a place to put our money. What kind of business do you run, Peter?"

"General merchandise. There's a lot of competition, but we seem to have an edge."

"How in the world do you run a business two thousand miles away? Aren't you afraid your customers and maybe even your employees will steal you blind while you're gone?"

Simpson laughed heartily. "Not a chance, my friend." He pulled a roll of paper tape from his pocket and, hand extended, showed it to his new acquaintance. "This tells me everything. It comes to me every day, straight out of a machine that tallies every sale."

70

Described as "a bit florid of countenance," John H. Patterson crafted his plans as carefully as his mustache. [NATIONAL CASH REGISTER CORPORATION]

Suddenly aware of a strange coincidence, the Massachusetts merchant hesitated a moment, then continued. "Strange," he said. "You come from Dayton, where I bought my little old money-saver from people in your town, the National Machinery Company. Ever hear of them?"

Patterson was silent for so long that Simpson wondered if he had offended him. When the former dealer in coal finally spoke, he said only, "Thank you, friend."

Hurrying back to his room, he told Frank of the unusual encounter in the lobby of the hotel. "Forget the cattle business," he insisted. "We're going home, and we're going to buy out Jake Ritty's company."

Jacob Ritty had no business experience before opening his café; he had been trained as a mechanic and thought he was getting into easier work when he switched to food service. Soon he found himself so worried about how much to buy and what to charge that he found it difficult to sleep. His doctor advised him to get his mind off the café, so he decided to make a trip to Europe in steerage.

Tired of being continuously crowded among other passengers, many of whom spoke no English, Ritty wandered into the engine room of the ship. He soon made friends with the chief engineer, returning to steerage only to sleep. One

The flip chart (then innovative) was John H. Patterson's trademark, here used under a tent at Sugar Camp. [NATIONAL CASH REGISTER CORPORATION]

day he noticed a strange contrivance making methodical movements and inquired its nature.

"It counts the revolutions of the propeller," the engineer explained. "Never misses, and makes a permanent record."

On the spot, Ritty had an inspiration. If a machine can count the revolutions of a propeller, he reasoned to himself, it ought to be able to count money in a café.

Back in Dayton and working with his brother, he soon developed a crude but workable device by which purchases could be recorded. But the National Machinery Company, organized for the manufacture and sale of Ritty's invention, did not prosper. Few saloon owners would even consider paying two hundred dollars for a machine they didn't think they needed, and barkeepers openly resented the idea of "having a machine to check up on us."

Grandson of a soldier who fought under George Washington before helping to found Cincinnati, John Patterson grew up on the family farm south of Dayton when the town's population was about ten thousand. He was an acceptable but not an outstanding student at Central High School. After finishing his term of enlistment as one of Abraham Lincoln's three-month volunteers, he earned a diploma from Dartmouth College.

Jobs were scarce, so John was glad to get a position as collector of tolls on one of several canals then in active use. When rent was deducted from his pay of ten dollars a week, he had just two dollars a week left. Because a boat could come at any hour of any day, he was on duty around the clock for seven days a week. To supplement his income, he hung out a sign offering for sale coal and wood, which he bought from a dealer only after he had found a purchaser.

Sometimes wondering why he had bothered to spend four years in college, he realized that he was following a dead-end road; there was no possibility of advancement. Therefore he borrowed $250 from a bank and with a brother bought a tiny retail coal yard, complete with a set of scales and two blind horses.

Complaints from customers led him to devise a system of receipts for both coal and cash, something radically new and different in the business. Gradually expanding until he was delivering half of the coal used in Dayton, he leased coal mines to boost his profit margin, then they bought three of them outright. Operation of a general store adjacent to his Coalton mine had shown him that an absentee owner was easily cheated. That big problem, he had said to Frank before they left Colorado, could be solved by the use of Ritty's machine, which kept an account of sales.

Patterson paid $6,000 for a controlling interest in the National Machinery Company, whose liabilities exceeded its assets. By now convinced that the device he was beginning to call the cash register would revolutionize commerce, he put all of his enormous energy and talent into the task of getting it into business places. By comparison with sales obstacles that often seemed insurmountable, production of the machine was a simple task managed by Frank.

Some of NCR's 15,000 employees in Dayton in 1911, with the manufacturing plant in the background. [NATIONAL CASH REGISTER CORPORATION]

It was the combination of man and machine—John H. Patterson and the cash register—that shaped the course of the emerging union between manufacturing and commerce. Although he has often been called "the father of modern advertising," Patterson was much more than that. His was the first business to offer salesmen exclusive rights to a territory, with their earnings to come from commissions only. The National Cash Register Company, as he called it soon after taking it over, was the first American manufacturing concern to establish a huge overseas market. If he was not the first person to use direct mail as a tool for mass marketing, he clearly was the man who showed it to be effective.

One of his early sales representatives, with headquarters in Indianapolis, turned in his resignation in disgust "because merchants don't want these mechanical monsters at any price." Patterson persuaded him to postpone quitting until he could "do a little spade work in the territory."

He assembled a list of five thousand merchants, then hired college students to address eighteen sets of envelopes. Each batch of envelopes having been stuffed with a different set of printed matter, he mailed five thousand each day for eighteen days and saw sales climb dramatically.

Brisk sales didn't end his financial problems because most purchasers paid in installments and he was buying one-fourth of all the two-cent stamps sold at the Dayton post office. During one gloomy month, cash on hand fell to ninety-one cents; he had three cents on hand in the office and an eighty-eight-cent credit at the bank.

That didn't stop John H. Patterson from moving into England, then crossing the channel into France, Germany, and Holland. Before his death in 1922, the man who had envisioned the cash register as a world-conquering machine reported that the German subsidiary had 1,000 employees, while a dozen other European countries accounted for 1,500 more.

Triumphant expansion based upon development of a training center for salesmen—complete with replicas of a saloon, a drugstore, and a grocery—was never unadulterated. When shipment after shipment of machines were returned from England and found to be defective, Patterson realized that he needed to pay attention to the needs of production workers. He immediately began making innovations designed to

Delivery of cash registers in Bombay, India, was even more spectacular than Patterson's delivery of coal by two blind horses. [NATIONAL CASH REGISTER CORPORATION]

bolster morale, and he regularly added new programs throughout his life. Perhaps the crowning touch was the creation of the National Cash Register Country Club, for use of which an employee and his family paid one dollar a year.

Scores of men who gained experience under Patterson moved on to other industries at the executive level. NCR was never a giant in terms of the money flow of Standard Oil, U.S. Steel, or Boeing, yet there was a long period during which one out of every six top corporate executives in the United States had learned the methods and attitudes taught by the founder of NCR.

Unlike most gifted entrepreneurs, Patterson never accumulated a personal fortune. He spent too liberally on civic and philanthropic causes to do so. Soon after his death, the family-held corporation went public but continued to make effective use of its founder's ideas while moving into the information age. NCR point-of-sale terminals in retail establishments now use laser techniques by which bar codes identify each product and record the price on the day of purchase. Main frame computers about the size of a suitcase and a range of personal computers are major products today, while services focus upon storage, transmission, and retrieval of information.

At the time NCR celebrated its one hundredth anniversary in 1984, president Charles E. Exley, Jr., emphasized that its role had been defined by the hand-operated cash register. In September 1991 AT&T and NCR merged to form a colossus within the information processing industry, which keeps Dayton a brightly lighted spot on the global map of commerce and industry.

The Patterson Homestead, 1815 Brown Street, Dayton, was built about 1816 by Colonel Robert H. Patterson, grandfather of the NCR pioneer. Colonel Patterson founded Lexington, Kentucky, as well as helped to establish Cincinnati. For information telephone (513) 222-9724.

PART THREE:
Pacesetters and Record Makers

John D. Rockefeller had the good fortune to move into petroleum very early, but without business acumen he would not have become the world's first billionaire. Had not Eddie Rickenbacker been influenced by the Wright brothers, he might not have been a veteran aviator before World War I. As in the case of Rockefeller, timing was only one factor among many that enabled Rickenbacker to set a record as the number one ace among fighter pilots of the conflict. From his boyhood in Ohio, Rickenbacker had shown uncanny manual dexterity, whose full import was not realized until he had downed his first dozen enemy planes.

Jim Thorpe had already made a world reputation when he came to Canton in 1919 to play football with the pre-NFL Bulldogs. He was later a Cleveland Indian and a Toledo Maroon before going to the New York Giants and coming back to Canton. Calling himself "a Buckeye by choice rather than birth," he was easily the greatest all-round athlete of his time. At the Olympic Games of 1912 he won both the pentathlon and the decathlon. Although Thorpe lost his medals because earlier he had played semi-pro baseball, his records stand, along with those of other Ohioans whose careers were as varied as their backgrounds.

Peter Thomson (**right**) *was welcomed to Washington in 1925 by President Calvin Coolidge* (**center**) *and Chief Justice William Howard Taft* (**left**), *another Buckeye.* [COURTESY CHAMPION INTERNATIONAL CORPORATION]

12

Peter Thomson Believed in Staying Ahead of the Pack

"Let's get things moving, I'm due at the office in half an hour."

Nodding understanding to his friend, Peter G. Thomson tapped on the table as a signal for quiet. Sturdy but so small that he was often described as diminutive, the Hamilton bookseller waved cigar smoke from his face without apology to those who were producing it.

"All of you know why you are here," he began.

"Sure! You need money! Any time you do, you turn to Cincinnati!"

"That's exactly right. I need enough, with what I already have on hand, to put $100,000 into a paper coating plant."

"Sounds risky to me," interjected one of the dozen business friends who had gathered at Thomson's request. "I can get all I want at a decent price. Looks to me as though the market is already saturated."

"You're right. It was already saturated on September 14, when vice president Theodore Roosevelt took over as president. But I'm here to tell you that it won't stay saturated very long. The new halftone process for printing photographs is so good that engravings and woodcuts are on the way out. But a print shop that turns out halftones can't use uncoated paper; the future for coated paper is limitless, gentlemen."

"What in blazes is a halftone?"

Thomson explained, "Photographers use what they call a screen. It turns a picture into a series of dots. They're evenly spaced, but their size varies according to the intensity of the tone they represent.

"To the eyes of a viewer, the resulting printed picture seems to be solid; spaces between the dots disappear. Until this process was developed, attempts to print photographs usually produced a very poor image, sometimes only a blob of black ink."

Most of the men present that morning had lent money to Thomson previously and had received prompt payment with full interest. A few were hesitant to advance large sums because he was considered to be a risk taker. Others thought that a person who never takes a risk can earn a good living but will never make big money.

By the time the impromptu gathering broke up, the bookseller and printer, who lived in Cincinnati but operated his business in Hamilton, had commitments enough to go ahead with his plans. In addition to capital for purchase of machinery and erection of a building, he'd have to pay wages of $3.50 a week to workmen.

With his formal schooling ending before his fifteenth birthday, Hamilton was shipping clerk of a bookstore at age twenty-one and had borrowed money to open his own store in 1877. After five years, when he found the profit margin to be lower than he had expected, he expanded into the printing business. Soon he was producing valentines and paper toys, along with what he called "the Triumph Noiseless Slate."

It was his decision to manufacture the slate that marked him as a risk taker. Even though chalk sometimes produced brief bursts of sounds when used on the Hamilton product, it was selling at the rate of two million per year by 1901. Tradition has it that success of his slate persuaded Thomson to look for innovations such as the halftone process and to try to find a way to profit from them.

Years later, he often told colleagues and employees that he had become wealthy as a result of following just two rules: "First establish good credit, then use it as much as you can. Second, remember that there's no such thing as succeeding through luck; the only sure way is to work hard."

By 1905 the prediction of the bookseller-printer who decided to go into manufacturing was proven accurate. The

*Thomson's printing establishment in Hamilton, spawned by a
starting business as a bookseller.* [COURTESY CHAMPION
INTERNATIONAL CORPORATION]

demand for paper coated with a mixture of clay and glue
mounted every year. Having moved into its production early,
the mill built with borrowed money produced a substantial
part of the total supply in the United States.

Thomson turned out so much coated paper that he sometimes was squeezed for above-market prices for uncoated
paper with which to work. That turned his eyes to Franklin,
Ohio, where he found and bought the Eagle Paper Company. Soon it proved inadequate for his needs, so he built a
paper-making mill at Hamilton.

To keep his paper-making machines in full operation, he

Some employees of Thomson's new coating mill in Hamilton. When it opened in 1898, top wages were one dollar for a ten-hour day. [COURTESY CHAMPION INTERNATIONAL CORPORATION]

needed a sure source of wood pulp at the right price. Having spent at least one vacation in Waynesville, North Carolina, he knew that the region had plenty of fine trees, water, and a dependable work force. So on the Pigeon River at Canton—named for Canton, Ohio—he put up a pulp mill owned by Champion Fibre Company, an Ohio corporation. Some of his competitors thought he was deranged, building a large plant in a North Carolina town with a population of three hundred. They didn't know that a large part of the $4.5 million needed to start the Canton enterprise was lent by William C. Procter, the head of the world's largest soap manufacturer, based in Cincinnati. In 1935 the Hamilton- and Canton-based operations combined to form the Champion Paper and Fibre Company.

By that time, the man whose career began as a shipping clerk in a bookstore had decided that producers of the clay used in coating paper were making a killing. So he turned to Sandersville, Georgia, where he bought a clay mine and erected a refining plant.

Long before research and development became so important to corporations that "R&D" entered popular speech, Thomson was encouraging his men to experiment. During World War I, probably under the leadership of his son-in-law Reuben B. Robertson, they made a major breakthrough by producing chlorine from salt water.

Soon the North Carolina mill, which long before had begun to produce finished paper, made news that caught the attention of the global business world. For the first time, printing paper of top quality was produced at the plant already boasting the world's fastest and most cost-productive paper-making unit.

It was at Canton that a special kind of cardboard was developed before 1935, while experiments with use of pine as a raw material were still under way. Using a special technique to coat cardboard with wax, the finished product not only proved to be sturdy, it was also bacteria free and just right for making containers for milk. When plastic was found to be superior to wax, a new coating plant was built at Waynesville, barely ten miles from the pioneer plant at Canton.

Reuben Robertson, whose career had started as a Cincinnati attorney, succeeded his brother-in law as head of the growing enterprise; then his son followed him. During fifty-seven years in which members of a single family presided over Champion, it continued to follow the simple formula of its founder: borrow and expand into new fields.

During twenty-five years in which one-third of the paper on which copies of *Life* magazine were printed on Champion paper, the company moved into the envelope business. Already it had gone international with a mill about one hundred miles north of São Paulo, Brazil.

The absorption of U.S. Plywood Company, with 19,000 employees, made the Hamilton-launched enterprise second in that market. An additional 43,000 employees were later added with the acquisition of Hoerner Waldorf, Inc., whose most familiar household product may be Waldorf toilet tissue. Part of the attraction of the Waldorf enterprise may have stemmed from the fact that it was a pioneer in recycling, long before that movement gained wide popular support.

Not all innovations were designed to boost profits. Environment-conscious Reuben B. Robertson arranged for a very unusual sale of 80,000 acres of prime spruce-growing land, the nucleus of today's Great Smoky Mountains National Park.

Peter G. Thomson didn't live to rejoice at the fact that timber land made available by his company launched the nation's most frequently visited national park. Neither did he survive to take pride in the fact that Champion spent $350,000,000 on internal improvements at the North Carolina plant during the 1990s. But long before his death, the Buckeye who believed in staying ahead of the pack took pride in having been the first to "go South" with major industry.

Canton is the burial place of the William McKinley family. The president and his wife lie in the center of the monument; their daughters, Ida and Katie, are interred in the walls.

13

Tecumseh Left a Lasting Mark upon America

"Pale warriors said I could not get past their fortified places, but here I am! In the great mountains, I have met with the Cherokee and found them to be brothers. Listen to me, today, Muskogee warriors!

"Spirits of the dead look down upon us and turn their heads. Listen! I hear their voices in the wailing wind! They believe we are cowards, because we have let the white man take our land. They want us to burn the spinning wheels and plows sold to us by the white man.

"Let us return to our old ways! Our friends, the British, will help us! O brothers of my mother, shake off the chains of slavery and rise up with the Shawnee and let us all reclaim our lands!"

Surrounded by twenty-four stalwart warriors smeared with war paint and wearing bonnets, the copper-colored orator, who had explained that they came from the place of the North Star, stalked to a position indicated by Big Warrior. With more than five thousand Muskogee tribesmen gathered for their annual grand council at Tuckabatchee, the conclave was crucial for Tecumseh's plans.

Sam Dale, the only white man present, recorded his impressions and jotted down much that Tecumseh said. Dale stood up in order to see more clearly as Big Warrior responded for all the tribesmen of half a hundred Creek towns in Alabama. Ponderously, the huge leader shook his head. "We cannot go with you now," he said. "We must have more time."

Enraged, Tecumseh let out what Dale described as "a most

Death of Tecumseh in the battle of the Thames in 1813.
[LIBRARY OF CONGRESS]

diabolical yell." Then he led his followers in a Shawnee war dance that was punctuated by the frequent scattering of tobacco and sumac. According to lore of the Shawnee, these potent herbs purified the ground and drove away evil spirits.

Watching impassively and seeming not to move a muscle, Big Warrior's stance clearly signaled that he had no interest in joining the war dance. Twirling before him and then coming to a stop, Tecumseh shouted defiantly, "Your blood is white!"

Turning to the followers of Big Warrior, the visiting Shawnee, whose mother may have been a Creek, pronounced a curse upon all white men. "You do not believe that I speak for Moneto, but I tell you that the Great Spirit has sent me!" he exclaimed. "You shall know. I leave you now. But when I am back at the Tippecanoe, I will stamp with my foot and shake the ground at Tuckabatchee!"

Just when and where the man whom whites called Tecumseh made his appearance is uncertain. He may have been born somewhere on Mad Creek, not far from present-day Springfield, but the great springs at Old Chillicothe (later Oldtown) may have been his birthplace. Nevertheless, he was a toddler at the time of Pontiac's Rebellion.

In 1774 his father, Pucksinwa, was killed in battle at Point Pleasant. Perhaps under the influence of his mother, A-Turtle-Laying-Her-Eggs-in-the-Sand, he grew up with fervent admiration for his racial past and its glories. His twin brother, Tenskwatawa, became revered as a prophet before he reached maturity. For his part, said the man whom many fellow Shawnees called Tikamthi ("Crouching Panther"), he wanted his tribesmen to return to the ways of their ancestors and stop giving land to white faces.

An outspoken advocate of peace until about age forty, Tecumseh encountered one person he vowed to kill some day. William Henry Harrison, as secretary of the Northwest Territory, had set out to silence all Indian claims to land. Made governor of the Territory of Indiana, Harrison concluded a number of treaties before deciding to launch all-out war against the Native Americans.

Somehow Tecumseh arranged to meet Harrison for a parley at which the Indian demanded the return of vast tracts of land taken from the tribesmen in return for token payments. When Harrison angrily refused, the Shawnee brandished his tomahawk and cried: "You took the land! They did not sell their country; why not talk of selling the air, the clouds, and the great sea [perhaps Lake Erie] as well as the land?"

Thwarted in his attempt to redress past wrongs or to stop the course of the white man's aggression, Tecumseh may have decided to follow the example of Pontiac. He set out on a long journey to the South where he hoped to strengthen the forces of allied tribesmen ready to fight for their land.

Puzzled and perhaps a bit awed by the man whom he had rebuffed, Harrison wrote of him:

> The implicit obedience and respect which the followers of Tecumseh pay to him is really astonishing and more than other circumstances bespeaks him one of those uncommon geniuses which spring up occasionally to produce revolutions and overturn the established order of things.
>
> If it were not for the vicinity of the United States, Tecumseh would, perhaps, be the founder of an Empire that would rival in glory Mexico or Peru. No difficulties deter him.

Tecumseh's difficult and dangerous journey through Kentucky, Tennessee, North Carolina, Georgia, Florida, and Alabama ended in disappointment when Big Warrior proved to be lethargic. Before the Indian leader could return to the village of Tippecanoe, Harrison and a band of soldiers struck it without warning.

Frontier tales glorified Harrison's encounter with the Native American as having been "the battle of Tippecanoe." Actually it was a minor engagement that was quickly won by the U.S. soldiers, but it boosted the prestige of the territorial governor so that he was sent to the White House by grateful voters.

Some of the medicine men present when Tecumseh was rebuffed by Big Warrior may have taken threats of the Shawnee seriously. Perhaps they watched the moon carefully until the time Tecumseh expected to be reunited with his brother. If so, they realized that by the white man's calendar the day Tecumseh threatened to shake the ground would be reached about the middle of December.

Thousands of white settlers who had never heard of Tecumseh were startled on December 16, 1811. Residents of Athens, Georgia, later said that although they were on solid

Seizure of Indian lands and victory in a minor military engagement elevated William H. Harrison to the presidency. [HARPER'S ENCYCLOPEDIA OF U.S. HISTORY (1905)]

ground, it seemed for a moment that they were aboard a ship rolling with the waves. Soon they discovered that some chimneys had cracked. Dishes rattled as far east as Augusta, Georgia, and on many farms the animals behaved strangely.

It was weeks before settlers in remote villages and towns learned that the United States had been hit by one of the most severe earthquakes of modern times. Aftershocks lasted until February 1812.

Centered close to New Madrid, Missouri, the first quake, and perhaps some of the later ones, would have registered close to the top of the scale had modern instruments been available with which to measure. An area of more than one million square miles was affected.

John James Audubon was riding his horse, Barro, in southern Kentucky on the fateful day. When the animal balked and spread his feet apart as though he feared he might fall, the veteran outdoorsman at first thought Barro might be dying.

Just as he started to spring from the animal's back, Audubon saw that "all the shrubs and trees began to move from their very roots, the ground rose and fell in successive furrows, like the ruffled waters of a lake, and I became bewildered in my ideas." Then he realized that "all this awful commotion in nature was the result of an earthquake."

Some observers insisted that for a time the Mississippi River flowed backward along part of its course, although there is no scientific confirmation of this report. However, the ground sank three to fifteen feet in an area eighteen miles long and five miles wide. Today the region permanently changed by the great earthquake of 1811 is a fast-growing resort area, Reelfoot Lake in Tennessee.

At the battle of Tippecanoe, one month before the great quake, William Henry Harrison defeated the Shawnees. But when the earth trembled as Crouching Panther had promised that it would, tribes allied under his leadership went on the offensive once more. Proudly wearing the uniform that identified him as a brigadier general in the British Army, "the warrior who stamped his foot to make the earth shake" was killed in the Canadian battle of the Thames.

*Tecumseh voices his opposition to torture of a white captive in the opening scene of the epic that depicts his life. ["*TECUMSEH*!"]*

William Henry Harrison's assessment proved to be accurate. Though dead, nothing could stop the spirit of "the Shawnee whose footprints can be seen at Reelfoot Lake." His name was passed along to a white man, William Tecumseh Sherman, who said, "War is hell"—and by his actions proved it to be just that. During the Civil War, the Shawnee leader was formally commemorated by the battleship USS *Tecumseh*.

Today he is the central figure in what many people regard as the best of outdoor historical dramas. Performed on Sugarloaf Mountain close to the former village of Chalah-gawtha—which gave Chillicothe its name—the epic is presented in a $1.5 million amphitheater. Use of eight separate stages permits players to ride through woodlands on horseback and to drive canoes over placid waters. Called by major newspapers "the spectacle that the others merely promise," the Chillicothe-based drama has a one-word title, *Tecumseh!*

Tecumseh! *is performed nightly, Monday through Saturday, from mid-June until early September. For information and reservations call (614) 775-0700.*

14

No Cannon Boomed during Benjamin Harrison's Biggest Battle

"Damn Benjamin Harrison! He is a cold-blooded, narrow-minded, prejudiced, obstinate, timid, old psalm-singing politician!"

That 1890 verdict from U.S. civil service commissioner Theodore Roosevelt was precisely opposite that of views expressed by farmers of Ohio, Indiana, and Illinois. Most of them were ecstatic in their praise of the man whom they correctly regarded as "the best friend we've had in the White House in years."

Political campaign literature of 1888 stressed that though William Henry Harrison had claimed to have been born in a log cabin, his grandson actually was. But soon after Benjamin made his appearance near North Bend in 1833, his grandfather had moved him and his parents to a splendid 600-acre farm.

His upbringing as a farm boy, who was seven years old when his grandfather was elected president, had a lasting impact upon Benjamin. Sniffing the air of Cincinnati from a distance, he denounced it as being foul and unwholesome. However, at age fourteen he went to the big city to study at Farmers' College preparatory school.

Credits earned there permitted Harrison to enter Miami University as a junior, where he met and soon married Caroline Lavinia Scott, daughter of the founder of the Oxford Female Institute. Nothing delighted the twenty-year-old bridegroom more than teaching Carrie about farming. Yet she was probably the person who persuaded him that he would have a better life as an attorney than as a tiller of the soil.

To those under whom he read law, Benjamin's high, soft voice didn't seem especially suitable for the courtroom. But his impeccable courtesy and reserve had already earned him the epithet of "human iceberg." Those traits could prove to be assets if he should ever be involved in a major legal contest.

For a few years such a course of events didn't appear likely. His career began as attorney for the city of Indianapolis at a salary of $400 per year, but within a generation his friendship with U. S. Grant put him squarely into the middle of a famous squabble.

Angry at having civil rights denied to him during the Lincoln administration, Lambdin B. Milligin sued army personnel for damages and was awarded $100,000. Then the 1866 case of *Ex parte Milligan* went to the U.S. Supreme Court for determination of the sum Milligan would actually recover. Convinced by Benjamin Harrison's reasoning, the high court awarded just $5 to Milligan.

Harrison had become acquainted with Grant during the years when both wore the blue uniforms of the Union army. At the outbreak of the Civil War, the Ohio-born attorney helped to raise the Seventieth Indiana Regiment and became a second lieutenant in the outfit. Month after month he spent helping guard the Louisville and Nashville Railroad from destruction by Confederates.

Rising slowly in rank during this period, Harrison—unlike many other officers—seemed to be satisfied with his duties. "I am not a Julius Caesar or a Napoleon," he confessed, "but a plain colonel with hardly as much relish for battle as for a good breakfast."

However, he later participated in some of the fiercest fighting of the Civil War. When the Atlanta campaign was launched, the brigade he then led was attached to Sherman's forces. Hence he fought his way down the red hills of north Georgia and into the city of Atlanta. Praise from General Daniel Butterfield boosted him to the brevet rank of brigadier general. He later followed Sherman into the Carolinas and saw destructive war at its vicious worst.

In 1888 Republican literature stressed that Benjamin Harrison (in contrast with his wealthy grandfather) actually was born in a log cabin. [CURRIER & IVES LITHOGRAPH]

Like many a Union army veteran, he found his uniform to be a sure source of votes—lots of votes. After service in the U.S. Senate he won the office earlier held by his grandfather. "No battlefield upon which my brigade found itself ever saw fighting so fierce as that I encountered as soon as I was established at 1600 Pennsylvania Avenue," he later said at an Ohio political rally.

There were many internal squabbles, as evidenced by the outspoken contempt expressed by Theodore Roosevelt, but Benjamin Harrison's biggest battle was fought on behalf of farmers whom he loved and with whom he identified.

A few days after having taken the oath of office, the new chief executive was visited by the secretary of state, James G. Blaine. Wasting no words, the cabinet member from Maine blurted out a warning: "Denmark has joined the enemy; all pork products from the United States are to be banned."

"Is Germany behind this move?"

"I'm afraid so. They claim our meat is tainted. It may be no more than a test of the willpower of a new president. But unless something is done, and quickly, American farmers will suffer badly. I hardly need to point out that when their income falls, the rest of the economy will suffer."

Benjamin Harrison nodded understanding. "Give me a few days to wrestle with the issue," he requested.

* * *

Under the president's leadership Congress passed the nation's first significant Meat Inspection Act, which included a provision giving the chief executive power to ban products of any nation that discriminated against U.S. exports. That provided Harrison with leverage in what threatened to become an all-out trade war. More than a century ago, the international contest had much in common with trade struggles in the 1990s between the United States and Japan over automobiles, auto parts, and electronic devices.

Germany sold huge quantities of beet sugar in the United States, Harrison learned. France, whose leaders had also erected high barriers against U.S. pork, shipped much of its wine to the West. Sugar and wine would soon face stiff tariffs, warned the man some called "a Buckeye iceberg," unless barriers toppled in Germany and in France.

Alone among chief executives, the man reared on an Ohio farm talked about pork in each of his four annual messages to Congress. An all-out trade war could have disastrous consequences, he confessed. Yet he used every weapon in the diplomatic arsenal to make his European trade adversaries capitulate. A master stroke comparable to bringing fresh

Campaign posters in 1888 exaggerated candidate Harrison's role in the Civil War. [LIBRARY OF CONGRESS]

Harrison and his men were in the thick of heavy fighting during the final Federal push into Atlanta. [THE ATLANTA CYCLORAMA]

troops to a battlefield came at the height of the struggle. Since a series of presidential prohibitions upon imports had not resolved the issue, Harrison engineered an agreement with Spain by which sugar from Cuba surged to new importance.

Much as one battered Confederate unit after another gave up the fight at Gettysburg under Federal fire, Germany, Denmark, and Italy repealed their restrictions on pork under pounding from Harrison. Austria-Hungary followed and finally the most stubborn enemy of all, France.

Benjamin Harrison's annual message of 1892 was triumphant. He had won the trade war against seemingly insuperable obstacles. Exports of pork to Europe had jumped by more than 50 percent. American raisers of hogs would have $20 million more to spend each year.

Never lauded as a victor upon a Civil War battlefield, former Major General Harrison had led Americans to victory against the world's strongest economic enemies of the U.S. farmer.

15

Harriet Beecher Stowe Hit Upon the Right Subject at the Right Time

Harriet Beecher Stowe, one of the most prolific of nineteenth-century American women writers, produced thirty-one books. Her novels range from *Pearl of Orr's Island* to *Agnes of Sorrento* and *My Wife and I*. She wrote widely for a juvenile audience, including *Betty's Bright Idea, Little Pussy Willow, First Geography for Children,* and *Queer Little People.*

She treated "domestic science" in *The American Woman's Home, The Chimney Corner,* and *House and Home Papers.* Largely because she correctly expected them to be profitable, she turned out nonfiction volumes dealing with *Men of Our Times, Our Famous Women,* and *Bible Heroines.* While producing a constant stream of books, she wrote magazine articles on subjects ranging from visiting Charleston, South Carolina, to dogs and cats and spiritualism.

Judged by exacting critical standards, *Uncle Tom's Cabin* is second-rate literature, but it is widely considered to be the most influential of all American novels. When published in a climate of fast-mounting sectional tension, its emotion-packed subject matter strongly appealed to ordinary readers.

Had Lyman Beecher's daughter Harriet remained in Connecticut where she was born in 1811, she might have died as a struggling writer. But in 1832 her father moved to what had once been "western Connecticut," taking her to Cincinnati where he founded the Lane Theological Seminary.

For the career of the woman who began dabbling with poetry and other forms of writing very early, the move could not have been better. As the self-proclaimed "capital of the West," Cincinnati had most of the cultural advantages of big

Harriet Beecher Stowe, tireless writer whose novel turned her into a reformer. [LIBRARY OF CONGRESS]

eastern cities. Three years after the Beechers arrived, its *Western Magazine* offered a fifty-dollar prize for the best story submitted, and the theological seminarian's daughter easily walked away with the honors.

She became active in the city's Semi-Colon Club, whose fellow members encouraged her to put her wildest fantasies on paper. She responded by penning a series of fictional letters that she wanted readers to believe were genuine.

According to her own account, when Harriet finished the first of these letters she went to great pains with the manuscript:

> I smoked it to make it look yellow, tore it to make it look old, directed it and scratched out the direction [or address], postmarked it with red ink, sealed it and broke the seal—all this to give credibility to the fact of its being a real letter.

Most folk were suspicious of fiction in general and novels in particular. This prevailing attitude probably accounts for the pains taken to make the bogus letter appear to be genuine. But when she became the second wife of Calvin Stowe, a professor in her father's seminary, Harriet's ambition was encouraged by her mate.

Calvin was no ordinary professor. His absorbing interest in improvement of education persuaded the state of Ohio to send him abroad to study European methods. But in his private life, he was a proper subject for what later came to be called gothic novels. Constantly in contact with the supernatural, he told Harriet that he once woke up to find an ash-colored skeleton in bed with him.

Calvin spent considerable time in the company of a very large invisible Indian woman and a small Indian man who played the bass viol. An especially vivid vision centered on a spirit named Harvey, who regularly squeezed between boards to enter Calvin's bedroom. Once he saw tiny fairies who danced with such abandon that he never forgot them. When he confided his secrets to his new wife, Harriet replied, "You must be of goblin origin!"

Had she married a man who would have scoffed at the notion of wasting time on fiction, her life might have been quite different. However, imaginary letter writers and characters conjured up by Harriet seemed tame, almost prosaic, by comparison with her husband's spirits.

Like him, she was intensely interested in educational reform. Like her father, she took a hands-off attitude toward the burning question of the day: abolition of slavery. But during the Cincinnati years in which she bore seven children, Harriet Beecher Stowe could not ignore the tensions created by those who wanted to do away with it.

Theodore Weld, one of her father's students, was so incensed at Beecher's middle-of-the-road views that he withdrew from school. Taking other students with him, he formed the nucleus of what became Oberlin College and wrote a passionate volume called *African Slavery As It Is*.

As the largest city situated between free and slave sections, Cincinnati was in constant turmoil. One of Weld's converts, James G. Fee of Kentucky, liberated his slaves and went home to preach abolition. He was run out of the state and disowned by his father.

135,000 SETS, 270,000 VOLUMES SOLD.

UNCLE TOM'S CABIN

FOR SALE HERE.

AN EDITION FOR THE MILLION, COMPLETE IN 1 Vol, PRICE 37 1-2 CENTS.

" " IN GERMAN, IN 1 Vol, PRICE 50 CENTS.

" " IN 2 Vols, CLOTH, 6 PLATES, PRICE $1.50.

SUPERB ILLUSTRATED EDITION, IN 1 Vol, WITH 153 ENGRAVINGS,

PRICES FROM $2.50 TO $5.00.

The Greatest Book of the Age.

Wood-engraved poster advertising Uncle Tom's Cabin, *produced in Boston in 1852.* [NEW YORK PUBLIC LIBRARY]

Another Kentuckian, Van Zandt, did not get off so lightly. When he freed his slaves and moved to an Ohio farm, he used it as a station on the Underground Railway. Authorities seized him, Harriet remembered in later life, "attached his property and threatened him with utter ruin." He escaped disaster only because he was represented in the courts by "a rising young Cincinnati lawyer, Salmon P. Chase," later U.S. secretary of the treasury.

Another of Weld's converts, identified by Stowe's wife only as Birney, came to Cincinnati to help edit an antislavery paper. When a mob destroyed his press, Harriet was so furious that she confided to Calvin: "I can easily see how such proceedings may make converts to abolitionism. I wish [Birney] would man [his building] with armed men, and see what can be done. If I were a man I would go, and take good care of at least one window."

In spite of strong emotional reactions against mob violence and awareness of the plight of slaves living just south of the Ohio River, Harriet Beecher Stowe was not an emotion-charged abolitionist. Instead she was a dedicated writer in search of a subject, which she found by turning back to her

Dozens of theatrical companies staged performances of Uncle Tom's Cabin *over a period of seventy years; a favorite theme for poster art was little Eliza's flight from "bloodhounds."* [MASSACHUSETTS HISTORICAL SOCIETY]

Cincinnati years after she accompanied Calvin when he moved to the faculty of Bowdoin College in Maine.

During a cold Maine winter, she began dabbling with a story that had slavery as the central theme. She embellished the story with her memories of the Bible and the novels of Daniel Defoe and Sir Walter Scott. Her first chapter described the death of a central character whom she called Uncle Tom, prompting novelist George Sand later to comment, "The life and death of a little child and of a negro slave!—that is the whole book!"

Her previous contacts with editor Gamaliel Bailey of Washington's *National Era* led her to be confident that he would publish her work as a serial. Harriet hoped to get enough money from *Uncle Tom's Cabin* to afford a new silk dress, and as late as July 9, 1851, she was working hard to publicize her story. In a letter to the noted black abolitionist Frederick Douglass, she ventured to hope that he might have seen early chapters of it. It was published in book form on March 20, 1852, shortly before the April issue of the *National Era* completed its serialization.

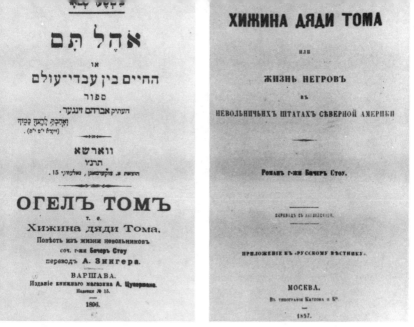

A Hebrew edition of Uncle Tom's Cabin (left) *appeared in 1896; a Russian edition* (right) *appeared in 1857.* [AUTHOR'S COLLECTION]

No one has ever succeeded in compiling an accurate account of the impact of the book and of stage plays based upon it. Before it was twelve months old, it had been translated into at least two dozen languages. When U.S. sales reached one million copies, admirers insisted that the author had established a record that "no other female will match for decades to come."

Throughout the Western world, celebrities praised the book and its writer; a letter from singer Jenny Lind was especially prized. England's Lord Shaftesbury sent her twenty-three morocco-bound volumes that held the signatures of 562,448 women who sent through Harriet "an affectionate and Christian address to the women of America."

Everyone knows that *Uncle Tom's Cabin* made an instant celebrity of its author, but she wrote dozens of other stories, articles, and books for financial reasons. Even the death of Calvin seemed a fit subject for two articles in the *Atlantic*, which she suggested to the editor "at my usual rates."

Her runaway best-selling novel turned Harriet Beecher Stowe into a reformer. Once the book was in hundreds of

Her Cincinnati home was never without at least one servant; so Harriet Beecher Stowe wrote books on "home management." [HARRIET BEECHER STOWE HOUSE]

thousands of American homes, she could no longer be moderate in regard to slavery. Hence she was vociferous in scolding Abraham Lincoln on two separate scores: He had never been known to read a novel, she correctly said, and his First Inaugural Address seemed insipid to the now-fervent crusader who never realized that Lincoln's dominant passion was preservation of the Union.

Widely circulated stories that Lincoln addressed the author of *Uncle Tom's Cabin* as "the little woman who started this big war" cannot be documented. Yet it was a conspicuous factor in helping to fan flames of sectional rivalry and hatred into a war that cost the lives of 623,000 fighting men. When the Civil War ended, the author, whose outlook had been transformed by her own handiwork, rejoiced not that the Union had been preserved but that slavery had been abolished.

Harriet Beecher Stowe's home still stands at 2950 Gilbert Avenue in Cincinnati; for information call (513) 632-5120.

In Ripley, the Rankin House State Memorial preserves the memory of an early abolitionist whose home was a station on the Underground Railroad. A refugee who stayed there after crossing the Ohio River on ice reputedly became Eliza in Uncle Tom's Cabin. *For information call (513) 392-1627.*

16

Thomas C. Eakin's Life Was Shaped in a Matter of Minutes

Early in the 1960s a famous man took the time to shake the hand of a teenage boy, inspiring him to achieve great goals. Most Americans have now seen camera footage of the brief meeting in the Rose Garden of the White House between President John F. Kennedy and young Bill Clinton.

A decade earlier, a notable in a different field gave his autograph to a high school junior and talked with him for several minutes at Cleveland's old Hollenden Hotel. That encounter with baseball superstar Cy Young helped to give direction to the boundless energy and contagious enthusiasm of seventeen-year-old Tom Eakin. One result of the meeting is the Ohio Baseball Hall of Fame on Key Street in Toledo's suburban Maumee.

Thomas Capper Eakin founded the institution and serves as its president. In the generations since Ohio was opened to settlers, only one Buckeye has had a day set aside in his honor in every county of the state. That happened in 1987 when Thomas C. Eakin Day was observed in every big city and most tiny villages.

Twenty years earlier baseball fans had set out to celebrate the centennial of Cy Young's birth in a memorable way. Who would be better to lead that effort than the man who had written regularly to the immortal sports figure at his Peoli home until his death in 1955? One glance at Eakin's collection of autographed pictures of Young was enough to convince any skeptic that he should be national chairman of the Cy Young Centennial. Before the two-day celebration ended in July 1967, Eakin was dreaming about ways to pay permanent

Thomas C. Eakin, inspired by record-setting Cy Young, proceeded to set quite different records of his own. [OHIO BASEBALL HALL OF FAME]

tribute to the man about whom he said, "My life was never the same after being touched by him."

Many times before, Eakin's sports promotion business had been temporarily set aside while he devoted his enthusiasm and energy to volunteer leadership of civic enterprises.

After having founded the Golf International 100 Club, Eakin continued as its president. Then he became founder-director of TRY (Target/Reach Youth) and the Interact Club of Shaker Heights. Earlier, he had launched and led the Rotary International student exchange club between the United States and Canada. Denison University graduates chose him vice president of the Cleveland alumni club.

He learned that enterprises he headed would survive and even thrive when benign neglect was mingled with imaginative leadership. Therefore, after he was recruited as a leader in the American Bicentennial celebration of 1975, he again turned his attention to the man whose humility and sincerity so impressed him during his adolescence. Using baseball memorabilia he had collected for many years as the

A rare postcard was issued when the baseball museum was located in Newcomerstown, not far from the home of Cy Young. [OHIO BASEBALL HALL OF FAME]

CY YOUNG MUSEUM

Ohio's Baseball Museum
Newcomerstown, Ohio

nucleus, Eakin established a nonprofit museum in New-comerstown, near Young's home. On dedication day, July 5, 1976, a number of great baseball players with strong Buckeye connections were inducted into the brand-new Ohio Baseball Hall of Fame.

Within five years the museum had outgrown its building and was honoring many notables of the diamond. That prompted a move to Springfield, followed three years later by a shift to still larger quarters within the Lucas County Recreation Center. At its new site the Ohio Baseball Hall of Fame and museum is next to Ned Skeldon Stadium, home of the Toledo Mud Hens. Cy Young memorabilia continue to pay tribute to the player who inspired the Hall of Fame. These include Young's 1904 perfect-game ball and photographs from his twenty-two-year major league pitching career that began in 1890.

From the old Cincinnati Red Stockings to today's Cleveland Indians, professional teams are represented. Although all inductees of the Hall of Fame have strong ties with Ohio,

Inductee No. 14, Cy Young (left), in the Baseball Hall of Fame readily admitted that he was the greatest player of all time, holding numerous pitching records unlikely ever to be broken. Larry Doby (right) joined the Cleveland Indians in 1947. As the first black player in the American League, in 1952 he led it in runs scored, doubles, and slugging percentage. In 1989 he became inductee No. 97. [OHIO BASEBALL HALL OF FAME]

the museum includes many mementos from "outsiders." Visitors not only can see what a Babe Ruth paycheck looked like, they can also determine how much he drew in two weeks. However, Buckeye memorabilia are spotlighted: Bill Wambsganss' 1920 World Series triple-play ball, the 1940 no-hit glove of Bob Feller, and the 1960 World Series glove and cap of Bill Mazeroski. Special baseball cards depict each member of the Hall of Fame and provide a capsule summary of his playing record.

With Hall of Fame inductees listed alphabetically, Cy Young's name is last on the list of more than one hundred players. Yet it is instantly apparent to a first-time visitor that memories of the Tuscarawas County farm boy dominate the place.

Born in Gilmore in 1867, the future baseball star was given the name Denton True Young, his middle name honoring a Civil War soldier who had saved his father's life in battle. Always called Dent by his family and friends, he stood six feet, two inches tall and weighed 200 pounds when his con-

Johnny Bench (left), inductee No. 105 in the Hall of Fame, became known as "the greatest catcher of all time" during sixteen years with the Cincinnati Reds. Hall of Fame inductee No. 78, Casey Stengel (right), managed the Toledo Mud Hens for five years and led the team to its first championship in the American Association. [OHIO BASEBALL HALL OF FAME]

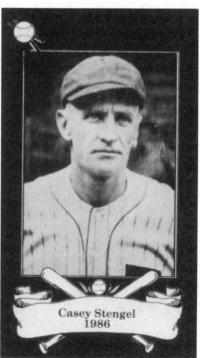

Johnny Bench
1991

Casey Stengel
1986

tract was bought in 1890 by the National League's Cleveland Spiders for three hundred dollars. Assigned to pitch against the Chicago Cubs, he was considered to be gawky and awkward—until he blistered the hands of a barehanded catcher squatting fifty feet away. Awed fans were amazed at "the cyclone from Tuscarawas" and dubbed him Cyclone Young. That nickname stuck to him for the rest of his life; abbreviated, it labels the coveted Cy Young Award that was established by baseball commissioner Ford Frick in 1956.

Young proved himself during his first two seasons with the Spiders. Yet in 1892 it was Cy to whom the Cleveland *Press* referred in a tongue-in-cheek baseball story. According to the story, persons living near the stadium at the beginning of the season "were startled by the violent trembling of the earth at exactly the same time that a big, fat farmer boy was trotting leisurely around the bases at League Park."

Laughter turned to adulation during the years in which Young pitched 7,377 innings in 906 games and won 511 of them—far more than a typical fan will ever see in a lifetime. His career as a big-league pitcher spanned so many other events that he scored a no-hit game during the presidency of fellow Buckeye William McKinley, then years later followed up with a similar win during the administration of another Ohioan, William Howard Taft.

He first racked up a no-hitter in 1897 against the Cincinnati Red Stockings, yet his salary never reached $5,000 a year. Playing in New York at age forty-one, he walked the lead-off man of his opponents on a 3–2 count. Once after Harry Niles was tagged trying to steal, Young retired twenty-six successive batters for an 8–0 victory.

During his career the distance between his box and the mound increased by ten feet, six inches, but that seemed to give Cy no trouble at all. He continued to deliver his famous "whistler" right under the chins of opponents during the twenty-two years in which he averaged pitching eight innings a game.

"Some of my cut-plug tobacco managed to get on the ball during early seasons," he later admitted. "That was when we used one ball for an entire game, which is why the 1904 perfect-game ball looks like it has been bounced around a greasy auto garage."

Every baseball fan knows that the one-time farm boy, whom some city slickers initially called Rube, set lasting records as the most successful pitcher who ever stepped up to a mound. With rules having been changed and longevity of careers reduced, the likelihood that anyone will ever surpass Cy Young is remote.

If the record-setting hurler were alive, he'd rejoice to know he inspired a teenager from his home state to make outstanding achievements.

Cy Young devotee Thomas C. Eakin became president of the Shaker Heights Rotary Club in 1970 at age thirty-seven. Emulating the pitcher whose records still stand, Eakin launched and completed twenty projects during twelve months to establish a Rotary International world record that has never been topped.

Since then he has received awards and commendations from Presidents Truman, Johnson, Nixon, Ford, and Reagan, as well as the Governor's Award, Ohio's highest. So many states and cities, governors, and mayors have paid special tribute to Eakin that his biographical listings have grown longer year by year. Editors of the *Guinness Book of World Records*, startled that he rated 128 lines in the forty-sixth edition of *Who's Who in America*, recognized him as having the longest entry of its sort ever. Yet the Guinness folk acted prematurely. In the 1992–93 edition of the same directory of achievers, fifty-nine-year-old Thomas C. Eakin's terse biography jumped to 142 lines.

Cy Young died at age eighty-eight; if he were around, he'd likely say, "Give that young fellow time, and he'll do so much that someone will some day establish a museum in *his* memory!"

17

A Perennial Failure at Thirty-seven, Pearl Gray Hit Pay Dirt in the West

"You don't seem to get around town much, my friend. How about going with me to hear Buffalo Jones talk about the Yellowstone?"

Alvah James touched the right button. His moody friend, a dentist who had practically abandoned his practice, surprised him by accepting instantly.

Members of the Campfire Club and their guests were intrigued by pictures the speaker showed. Nicknamed Buffalo because of his crusade to save the fast-vanishing big animals, Charles J. Jones owned land on the rim of the Grand Canyon. His talk about the West so intrigued Pearl Gray that the dentist did something unusual: he told a new acquaintance that he'd like to go home with him to spend a few weeks.

That 1907 visit to Arizona, punctuated by brief excursions into Utah and Colorado, was later seen as the turning point in the life of the New York professional who had grown up in Ohio. He had worked extremely hard for years at free-lance writing but with no success. However, he had recently read the novel *The Virginian,* and he thought in the untamed adventureland of the West surely he could find background information and characters to help him produce a good western novel.

As a boy in Zanesville, Pearl preferred fishing and baseball to school work. Classmates teased him so much about his unusual name that he stormed into the house one day and demanded: "Mother, why on earth did Queen Victoria's pearls seem so important to you? One of these days, I'm gonna get rid of the name you gave me in honor of her!"

Years later, he did, calling himself by his middle name, Zane. Simultaneously, he altered the spelling of his last name from Gray to Grey.

But it was Pearl Gray who had kept a fishing pole in the Muskingum River until dark any evening he didn't have a baseball game scheduled. Though not quite rebellious, he resented having to go to school and having to obey his parents. Most of all, he recalled in later life, he hated having to stand close to his father and fan flies away from his face as he dozed.

Reading was different, almost as much fun as fishing or throwing a ball. Pearl devoured most of the dime novels sold in the town of 10,000 and became enamored with Jesse James and Buffalo Bill, especially Buffalo Bill. Then he read and reread James Fenimore Cooper's *The Last of the Mohicans* around the time his family moved to Columbus.

Long before he was ready to put his fishing pole and *The Last of the Mohicans* aside, his father informed him, "Now that you're half-grown, son, it's time for you to help me out."

Pearl suspected what Lewis Gray meant, even before he went into details. A self-taught dentist, his father was increasingly troubled by arthritis, which was causing his performance to decrease and his income to drop. For weeks he had been considering offering dental service one day a week in outlying towns.

At age eighteen Pearl boarded the train to Frazeysburg for his first day as a dentist. Following his father's instructions, he did nothing but pull teeth with a shoulder, arm, and hand made strong by years on the baseball field. Soon teenage girls were coming to Frazeysburg to have their teeth examined, whether they were damaged or not. That led first to cleaning and then to filling by "young Dr. Gray."

When the Ohio Dental Association found out what was going on, officials closed Pearl's office and advised him to spend a few years in the study of dentistry, a profession that didn't really interest him. At the University of Pennsylvania he received cheers at baseball games but scowls from his professors who grudgingly gave him barely passing grades.

Someone on the staff of the dental school told him he'd

A Treasury of Ohio Tales

have a hard time of it in a small town; too many dentists were already established in them. Since he had been advised to begin his practice in a city, Pearl picked the biggest of them all, New York. He hung out his shingle at 100 West 74th Street a few months after his twenty-fourth birthday.

As a big city dentist, Pearl was a disaster. Many patients sensed that he didn't have his heart in his work. Others reported for scheduled appointments only to find the office closed because Dr. Gray thought the fish might be biting in a nearby river.

He devoted many nights, as well as weekends and times when the office was closed all day, to reading and writing. Often he'd spend an hour or two with Daniel Defoe or Robert Louis Stevenson, then pull out a sheaf of paper and begin scribbling or revising a story about fishing or hunting.

He haunted offices of magazine editors and came to know many of them well, but he seldom got encouragement about stories that bore the name of P. Zane Grey. One editor later offered a tentative explanation.

"Some of the stories had merit," he confessed. "But Zane refused to use a typewriter, an attitude that never changed. Maybe it somehow reminded him of the dental devices he despised. Manuscripts offered in longhand were usually put on the bottom of the slush pile and were never read."

For a few weeks in 1902 the aspiring writer was elated when *Recreation Magazine* promised to publish his piece about "A Day on the Delaware." Subject to mood swings that alternated between profound depression and joyous ecstasy, Zane was sure that at age thirty he had finally reached his goal and could give up dentistry for good.

But rejection after rejection followed as he continued to submit poems, articles, and stories to magazines in every major city of the Northeast. Except for a short article in a 1903 issue of *Field & Stream*, his name did not again appear in print until the same magazine published a four-page piece on fishing in 1906.

By then he had met and married Lina Elise Roth, whom he called Dolly. She had come to him as a dental patient, listened to him tell of his yearning to become a published writer, and encouraged him to keep trying. Long before they married, she mentioned that she was expecting "a nice inheritance" from her grandfather. There would be no better way to spend it, she told her dentist, than to help an aspiring writer.

Swinging into exultant high gear, Zane turned to his own background. Drawing upon the story of Fort Henry and his ancestor Betsy Zane, he churned out a full-length novel, *Betty Zane*, which was published in 1903. Even after achieving fame, he was always extremely reticent about his early novels, but it appears that Dolly's inheritance paid for the publication of at least three.

His brief trip to the West with Buffalo Jones inspired him to write *The Heritage of the Desert*. Refusing to admit that he was a failure at age thirty-seven, he submitted it to both Harper's and Street and Smith's. When published the following year by Harper's at $1.35, it was modestly successful. More importantly, it established a pattern he was destined to follow for the rest of his life.

By the time he paid a long visit to Zanesville in 1921, Zane Grey was a literary celebrity, author of *Riders of the Purple Sage, Wildfire,* and *The U.P. Trail,* as well as a book on fishing and many articles and stories in major magazines. Unyielding tenacity, ceaseless self-study, and Dolly's money had produced a literary phenomenon.

Inordinately proud of his trace of Indian blood, he was an early crusader for rights of Native Americans. Long before ordinary people became conscious of ecology, he advocated preservation of our natural heritage. Because he felt military veterans were not getting their due, he sparred with two U.S. presidents, Calvin Coolidge and fellow Buckeye Warren G. Harding.

No one knows how much material Zane produced; scores of pieces published by magazines were never used in books. Some estimates place his output—always handwritten—in the range of ten million words. Of his eighty-nine books, his fifty-six novels of the West have been reprinted and translated most often. Nationwide, small-town libraries include one hundred or more of his books.

Having established himself as one of the most sought-after writers of his time, Grey lived to see many of his books purchased by Hollywood producers, sometimes for two, three, or more film versions. Since his death in 1939, works of the Zanesville native have been the source of hundreds of hours of television.

Ex-dentist Zane Grey established a record as the most widely read novelist to write about the West; and he did it in his final thirty years, substantially less than half of his life.

Many of Grey's personal belongings and copies of his manuscripts may be seen during March through November at the museum honoring him near Zanesville. For information call (614) 872-3143.

18

Billy Gable Got a New Name and a Set of Store-bought Teeth

Will Gable, a wildcat oil driller who ran a small farm to put food on the table, drifted into Cadiz, Ohio, shortly before the death of William McKinley put Theodore Roosevelt into the White House. He was away from his home there, working in a Pennsylvania oil field, when his son and namesake was born.

Billy's mother had a hard time with her delivery; it seemed to make her epilepsy worse. She never recovered from childbirth, lingering for seven months before she died. Grandparents looked after the baby for more than a year; then Will married a milliner and set up housekeeping again, this time in Hopedale.

Jennie Dunlap, Billy's stepmother, loved him as though he were her own flesh and blood. She reared him tenderly and took so much pride in him that she was on hand to watch when he graduated from Hopedale School. A few months later as he prepared to enter Edinburgh High, she warned him several times: "Stay away from that Andy Means. Folks in Cadiz say he bears a lot of watching."

That seems to have pushed Billy into making the baseball team—just so he could spend a lot of time with Andy. Near the end of their junior year, Andy raced across the school yard one morning, gesturing for his friend to meet him.

"What I told you yesterday was right," he began. "Tire plants in Akron are hiring again. You're six feet tall and weigh 150 pounds; it's time for you to cut the apron strings. I'm going to Akron, and I want you to go with me."

Billy hesitated briefly. He had never been sixty miles away

from home; if he got to Akron and didn't like it, he'd find it hard to come all that way back. Soon, though, he agreed. Whatever he might find in Akron, it had to be a lot better than Hopedale.

Andy's information was correct, and both boys were hired at the first tire plant they approached. Although the pay was good, Billy found the work as monotonous as it was tiresome. He had come to the city for adventure, not to work himself to death. Since he had to eat, he kept his job; but at the local music hall, the manager of a little stock company offered him some excitement. He could become a backstage call boy, he was told, if he'd work for nothing, even though he needed two more years to graduate from high school. Billy hadn't worked a week before he decided that the stage was the place he wanted to be. Having tasted the heady wine of the theater, he never lost his appetite for it, not even during the time he reluctantly spent in the Oklahoma oil fields with his father.

At twenty-one he inherited $300 from his grandfather and turned toward Kansas City, vowing that he'd never again work twelve-hour days in anyone's oil field. Bedraggled in dress, still grimy with oil, and badly in need of a visit to a dentist, Billy talked his way into a traveling theatrical group whose members called themselves the Jewell Players.

When the players ran out of money in Montana, Billy was so disheartened that he decided to take any job he could find and forget the theater. He worked at sawmills, sold ties in a department store for a few months, then took on odd jobs for a newspaper. He was working for a telephone company when he heard that a woman who had performed on Broadway was getting ready to organize a theatrical company.

Josephine Dillon was patient with Billy, so patient that some members of her company charged that she was showing preference to him. In turn, he thought she was the most beautiful woman he'd ever seen. So the lovesick young fellow from Ohio followed her when she moved to Hollywood in 1924. In the last month of the year they were married, although he was fourteen years her junior.

"I can get you parts as an extra," she promised her hus-

Clark Gable as Rhett Butler and Vivien Leigh as Scarlett O'Hara in Metro-Goldwyn-Mayer's Gone With the Wind.

band, "but you'll have to stop being called Billy." That's how the native of Cadiz started using his middle name and introduced himself to casting directors as Clark Gable. Shortly afterward, concerned about his appearance, Josephine persuaded a director to provide her husband with a good set of dentures. Thus the devilish grin, which became his trademark, was made possible by flashing porcelain teeth.

There followed four Broadway productions, only one of which, *What Price Glory* in 1924, was a success. Then came a divorce from Josephine and the formation of a friendship with actor Lionel Barrymore, who helped him get a part in a road company that stopped in Houston, Texas, where he caught the eye of Ria Langham. Having profited handsomely from each of her three divorces, she had the money to see that Clark began dressing like a wealthy gentleman—complete with spats, cane, and derby. Already, he jokingly liked to call himself The King, and Ria saw to it that he looked the part. Seventeen years his senior, she became his second wife. Later he married the glamorous film star Carole Lombard who was tragically killed in a plane crash during World War II. After a short fourth marriage to Sylvia Hawkes, at the time of his death in 1960, he was married to the former Kay Spreckles, who was the mother of his only child, a son.

Moving to Hollywood, the self-styled "King" appeared in bit parts before Metro-Goldwyn-Mayer offered him a contract for more money than he had ever earned in his life—$350 a week. The head of the studios, Irving Thalberg, told colleagues that he sensed something extraordinary in Gable. As a result, the obscure actor soared to stardom in *The Painted Desert* in less than a year. Clark's salary was boosted to $2,500 a week, then to $4,000.

Flashing the smile that had become famous, this man from Ohio was among the earliest of celebrities to cause near riots when he visited cities such as Baltimore and Kansas City. Hundreds of women formed long queues before his dressing room. A few ripped off their bras and asked him to autograph them; others tried to persuade him to father their children.

Just seven years after having taken Hollywood by storm, Clark Gable put his footprints into the sidewalk near Grauman's Chinese Theatre. He made such memorable movies as *It Happened One Night* (1934) and *Mutiny on the Bounty* (1935). Then came his most famous performance as Rhett Butler in *Gone With the Wind* (1939). For more than two decades the high school dropout from Cadiz reigned as The King of Hollywood, one of the world's best-known personalities.

PART FOUR:
A Badly Divided State
Reflected the Divided Nation

During the Civil War, more than 350,000 Buckeyes fought in blue uniforms, and the two most influential Union generals came from the state. In addition to U. S. Grant and William T. Sherman, Ohio sent to war Philip H. Sheridan, Irvin McDowell, George A. Custer, William S. Rosecrans, Don Carlos Buell, James B. McPherson, James A. Garfield, and William McKinley.

Civilians Salmon P. Chase and Edwin M. Stanton were key advisers of Abraham Lincoln, while Senators Benjamin Wade and John Sherman helped to determine the course of congressional actions.

Yet it was Ohio that produced Clement L. Vallandigham, the most outspoken and influential of all "Peace Democrats." During some crucial years, Democrats controlled the congressional delegation.

War fostered the rise of partisan bodies not under direct military control; of the dozens that made life miserable for their foes, the pro-South band led by William C. Quantrill of Ohio was the most brutal. So many Copperheads called Ohio home that stern measures were taken to suppress their activities.

Ohio was for more than four years a microcosm of the divided nation, reflecting all the tensions and animosities that led the North to make war upon the seceded South.

Clean-shaven president-elect Abraham Lincoln as depicted for readers of a British newspaper. [ILLUSTRATED LONDON NEWS (DECEMBER 8, 1860)]

19

Ohio's Split Delegation Put Candidate Lincoln over the Top

Members of the Ohio delegation to the Republican National Convention huddled close together in Chicago's cavernous Wigwam. Joseph Medill, publisher of the Chicago *Tribune*, shoved his way toward them through packed aisles and called, "Please let me in; I must speak with your chairman."

One delegate cried, "No!" But others moved aside, wondering at what might be going on.

Medill reached leather-lunged David K. Cartter, leaned over, and spoke to him so cautiously that men close by were unable to hear what he said. Cartter then whispered to Medill, whose head nodded up and down vigorously in response.

Jumping to his feet, the Buckeye political leader cried at the top of his voice, "Mis-ter Chair-man!"

Banging of the gavel did not restore order to the noise-filled Wigwam, but the signal was clearly understood to mean that Cartter had the floor.

Climbing upon the seat of his chair, the man from Ohio waited for a moment and managed to get the attention of hundreds. "Mis-ter Chair-man!" he repeated. "The great state of Ohio wishes to announce the change of four votes from Mr. Chase to Mr. Lincoln!"

Murat Halstead of the Cincinnati *Enquirer* later informed his readers: "There was a noise in the Wigwam like the rush of a great wind in the van of a storm. Then, in another breath, the storm was there. Thousands cheered with the energy of insanity."

Said the veteran journalist: "Many thrust fingers into their ears to stop the pain produced by frantic, shrill, and wild shouting. No Comanches, no panthers ever struck a higher note, or gave screams with more infernal intensity."

Hundreds yelled themselves hoarse because they knew Cartter's announcement meant that the youthful Republican party had a nominee for the presidency. With Democrats divided into three camps, Lincoln of Illinois was virtually guaranteed the White House—and thousands of Republicans could expect to be rewarded with federal jobs.

Earlier, Buckeye politicians had been surprised when they learned that the Illinois State Convention had nominated Abraham Lincoln of Springfield. Along with many Republicans from other states, they were under the impression that Illinois would not place a favorite son in nomination.

Had national committee member David Davis not made just such a promise, the convention never would have gone to Chicago. Once the site was picked, the bustling city built the first structure ever designed to accommodate a national political convention. Repudiating the pledge given by Davis, Republicans of the state voted to offer Lincoln as a homespun "rail splitter candidate of all the people."

William H. Seward of New York, long nationally known as Mr. Republican, was expected to score an easy win in Chicago. But as convention time approached, it became clear that some of his support was soft. Ohio leaders doubted that he could carry the Northwest, which was crucial to victory.

Also, they had not one candidate to offer, but two. Veteran senator Benjamin Wade had a strong following among radicals who were on record as willing to do anything to abolish slavery.

Ex-governor Salmon P. Chase, recently elected to the U.S. Senate by the legislature, was favored by moderates who hoped to see sectional compromise that could avert civil war. David D. Field and Hiram Barney of New York made no secret of their preference for Chase. Because he had scattered support in other states as well, he was generally considered to be second only to Seward in strength.

Chicago's huge Wigwam as it appeared at the time of the Democratic National Convention in 1864. [HARPER'S WEEKLY (SEPTEMBER 3, 1864)]

Badly divided but having 46 votes to cast, most Ohio delegates reached Chicago on Saturday, May 12. With chairman Cartter presiding, they spent hours in hot debate. To some the idea of a unit vote by which every Buckeye delegate would support a single nominee made a great deal of sense. But followers of Chase were suspicious. If such a policy were adopted and a majority should decide to go for Wade, Chase would be left without sufficient support. After two stormy sessions in which the unit vote failed to be adopted, it was clear that each delegate could and probably would vote for the candidate of his own choice.

Robert E. Paine of Cleveland, leader of the Wade faction, had urged that only his man could win Pennsylvania's 54 votes. Ben Eggleston of Cincinnati argued that strong foes of slavery would never work to put Chase into the White House; he was considered to be on the fence and unwilling to back the use of force to free the slaves of the Cotton Belt.

Aware that they had gathered to take the first step in a

process that would almost certainly lead to election of a president, Republicans were called to order on Wednesday, May 16, to attend to preliminary business. A platform was adopted the following day, but the surprising discovery that printed ballots were not ready forced postponement of the first vote until Friday morning. Only a few insiders then knew that "failure of printers to deliver as promised" was due to work of the Lincoln faction.

The roll call of states, then being done geographically beginning with New England, clearly gave Seward a chance to win the necessary 233 votes on the first ballot. But he fell 59½ short, partly because 34 of Ohio's votes went to Chase. Just as Wade's followers had predicted, Pennsylvania abandoned Seward on the second ballot and threw its weight behind Lincoln. As a result, Seward picked up only 11 new votes, while Lincoln gained 79.

With Lincoln and Wade considered by some to be the only two former Whigs from the Northwest who would be acceptable to abolitionists, half a dozen members of the Ohio delegation got busy. They fanned out through the Wigwam, passing out hastily printed handbills that proclaimed:

> Honest-to-God statements by the Hon. Abraham Lincoln of Illinois, made at Springfield, Ohio, on the sixteenth day of September, 1859:
>
> Anything that argues me into the idea of social and political equality with the negro, is but a fantastic arrangement of words by which a man can prove a horse chestnut to be a chestnut horse. I have no purpose directly or indirectly to interfere with the institution of slavery in the States where it now exists. I have no lawful right to do so and I have no inclination to do so. I have no purpose to introduce political and social equality between the white and the black races.

Aware that many who listened to him in Columbus, Dayton, and Cincinnati had strong economic ties with the South, Lincoln hoped to avoid offending them. He failed to realize that voters of Ohio were already divided into moderate and radical camps, with the latter committed to Wade and willing to hurt anyone who seemed to be standing in his way. With

William H. Seward, "Mr. Republican," lost support because his views about slavery were well known, while Lincoln's were not. [LIBRARY OF CONGRESS (BRADY STUDIO PORTRAIT)]

Seward clearly in trouble, distribution of the handbills in Chicago was calculated to foster the "Stop Lincoln!" movement and bring Wade to the forefront.

Events soon showed that it was too late to try to stop Lincoln. Throughout the Wigwam, veteran politicians agreed that "a swing was on." That verdict proved to be accurate when the third ballot was tallied. Seward had lost only 3 votes, but Lincoln had surged to a total of 231½, just 1½ short of nomination. It was at this dramatic moment that the hurried Medill-Cartter conference led to the announcement of the changed votes that put Lincoln over the top.

Cartter never revealed what Medill told him at the crucial moment. Angry that Salmon P. Chase was being talked about as U.S. secretary of state, some of his associates accused Cartter of having betrayed Wade. They did not then know that Lincoln's campaign manager had promised to reward Ohio for her support, causing Chase to enter the cabinet as secretary of the treasury.

Senator Benjamin Wade lost to Lincoln in Chicago and later headed a congressional committee that made life miserable for the president. [NICOLAY AND HAY, *ABRAHAM LINCOLN*]

Regardless of what trades took place and what promises were made and altered, Ohio had the honor of making Lincoln the nominee and the next president of the United States. Followers of Chase were far from satisfied with what had taken place, and many adherents of Wade were downright angry.

Reactions by Ohio delegates did not affect the deed already done, and so men from other states quickly jumped on the bandwagon and began switching their votes. By the time Seward's floor manager moved to make the nomination unanimous, dozens of delegates had left the Wigwam.

If many who were present on that momentous day soon forgot the name of the man whose announcement took Lincoln over the top, the new president did not. On November 3 he asked the Senate to confirm David K. Cartter as his choice for U.S. minister to Bolivia. Later, facing the likelihood of defeat in his 1864 bid for re-election, Abraham Lincoln finished paying his debt to otherwise forgotten Cartter by making him chief justice of the Supreme Court of the District of Columbia.

20

Unarmed Civilians Ambushed General Sherman

A truce is to be observed by all parties. Confederate armies are to be disbanded and conducted to their State capitals, there to deposit their arms and public property in the State Arsenal . . . to be used solely to maintain peace and order within the borders of the States.

All Federal Courts will be re-established in the several states.

People of all the States are to be guaranteed, so far as the Executive can, their political rights and franchises as well as their rights of person and property.

Considerably abbreviated, these paragraphs formed the heart of an agreement signed near Durham's Station, North Carolina, on April 18, 1865. W. T. Sherman, major general and commander of the U.S. army in North Carolina, used the pen first. J. E. Johnston, the general commanding the army of the Confederate States in North Carolina, then added his signature.

Robert E. Lee having earlier surrendered at Appomattox, Johnston's capitulation meant the end of the 1,400-day Civil War. The complete text of the agreement was sent to Washington by telegraph, and soldiers of both forces engaged in riotous revelry that the killing was finally over. Southerners were elated by the promise of a quick return to normal conditions in their once-seceded states.

Their exuberance proved to be premature. General U. S. Grant reached Raleigh on April 24. Obedient to the demands of U.S. secretary of war Edwin M. Stanton, Grant notified Sherman to terminate the truce and to resume hostilities "at the earliest moment you can."

*   *   *

Sherman's grandfather, Judge Taylor Sherman, had reached Ohio's Western Reserve as a surveyor of land to be given to veterans of the Revolution. He was paid for his services in land, and his son Charles left Connecticut for the West. Initially planning to settle at Zanesville, the attorney whose family was rapidly increasing in size turned toward Lancaster in Fairfield County. When his son William was born there, Charles Sherman insisted that Tecumseh be added to his name as a tribute to the great Native American warrior. Members of his immediate family found Tecumseh to be unduly long, so they called the boy Cump.

At his death in 1829, Cump's father left ten children, three of whom were old enough to look after themselves. But it was necessary to divide the rest among acquaintances willing to take one or two poverty-stricken orphans. Cump, age nine, went into the household of prosperous and influential Thomas Ewing, who became a U.S. senator in 1831.

Soon Senator Ewing arranged an appointment for Cump at the U.S. Military Academy. After graduating from West Point, where some of his fellow cadets called him Chump, he spent thirteen years in uniform before returning to civilian life. For almost five years he was stationed in the South. At Fort Moultrie in Charleston, he met Robert Anderson of Kentucky, who was destined later to play a central role in transforming sectional strife into warfare.

Riding his horse across much of northern Georgia and Alabama, Cump gained first-hand knowledge of the land across which he later led his army toward Atlanta. Oral tradition says that he became enamored with Cecelia Stovall, who lived near Cartersville, Georgia, but upon his return to Ohio he married Ellen Ewing, his foster sister.

They were in Louisiana when it became clear that civil war was about to start. Serving as superintendent of a shool that evolved into Louisiana State University, Sherman was offered a Confederate commission. He turned it down, then rejected a Federal commission because he believed Lincoln's call for 75,000 ninety-day volunteers was hopelessly inadequate.

Having no political aspirations, William T. Sherman succeeded Grant as commander of all U.S. armies. [J. C. BUTTRE ENGRAVING, AUTHOR'S COLLECTION]

Later Cump donned his uniform again and served for a time as an aide to his old friend Anderson, now a brigadier general. He was blamed for ineffective leadership before Shiloh and at Chickasaw Bluffs, but he never suffered a major defeat. Enjoying the full confidence of Grant, he was put in command of the campaign designed to capture Atlanta. The fall of the city led to observance of a day of thanksgiving throughout the North. Abraham Lincoln had special reasons to rejoice; Sherman tipped the scales in the hotly contested presidential campaign of 1864 and helped return his commander in chief to the Executive Mansion.

Cump's subsequent March to the Sea is widely regarded as the first campaign fully to employ "modern warfare" designed to break the morale of the enemy. He presented the city of Savannah to Lincoln as a Christmas gift, then turned north toward "the seed bed of secession."

Whether or not he personally played a role in the burning of Columbia, South Carolina, is still debated. His systematic destruction of railroads and factories and his pillaging of towns and farms is not. Looting by his "bummers" caused the red-haired general to become one of the most hated of

Civil War leaders well before he reached North Carolina in quest of the last significant Confederate army.

Joseph E. Johnston, who had left a high post in the U.S. Army to fight for the Confederate States of America, had retreated slowly and skillfully. However, when he learned of Lee's surrender, he realized that the position of his army was untenable. He agreed to meet Sherman during the third week of April because he saw that more slaughter would accomplish nothing and because he was confident that the man from Ohio would make possible an honorable surrender. It was the specific terms upon which the two graduates of West Point agreed—not the issue of Confederate surrender—that triggered violent reactions in Washington.

Trouble stemmed in part from the assassination of Abraham Lincoln. Word of the tragedy reached North Carolina after a preliminary agreement had been reached but before the final papers were signed. To the surprise of Sherman, newspaper reporters said that U.S. secretary of state, William H. Seward, had also been a target of the gang led by John Wilkes Booth. Under fuzzy precedents about presidential succession, had the attempt upon Seward succeeded, only Vice President Andrew Johnson would have blocked Edwin M. Stanton's path to the Executive Mansion.

To this day, some analysts believe that the secretary of war played a behind-the-scenes role in the assassination plot. That is debatable, but his thirst for power is not. He was ready to sacrifice anyone and anything that stood in the way of his personal ambition. William Tecumseh Sherman was just such a person. Immensely popular as a result of his sweeping military victories, Sherman was widely regarded as a likely candidate for the presidency as soon as hostilities ceased.

Reporters and editorial writers who urged readers to help make him the nation's chief executive wrote without having consulted him. Sherman repeatedly and emphatically made it clear that he wanted nothing to do with the presidency or any other political office. Stanton may not have been aware of this announced stance. Whatever the case, he saw an oppor-

U.S. secretary of war Edwin M. Stanton, aspirant for the presidency. [BATTLES AND LEADERS]

tunity to put Sherman through an ordeal of public humiliation. Consulting the former vice president whom tragedy had elevated, Stanton succeeded in having cabinet members called together.

President Johnson and seven advisers gathered at the Executive Mansion to decide what to do with the man who had accepted Johnston's surrender. Seizing upon Sherman's reference to "rights of person and property" on the part of defeated Confederates, the secretary of war pointed out that slaves were property. "He drafted these terms in order to preserve slavery and to re-establish governments of seceded states," Stanton insisted.

Eight unarmed civilians gathered at 1600 Pennsylvania Avenue obediently backed Stanton in preparing an ambush for the general second only to Grant in esteem among Northern voters. They agreed to rescind Sherman's generous terms, then sent Grant to take over Sherman's army, an order that Grant ignored.

Except for Lincoln's assassination and Lee's surrender, no Civil War event received newspaper coverage equal to that devoted to the humiliation of William Tecumseh Sherman. Had he harbored any political aspirations, his hopes would have been dead; Stanton's plan to remove him as a possible rival worked perfectly.

Even the secretary of war could not, however, take from the Ohio native the glory he had won in his southern campaigns. He had to be included when plans were made for a two-day victory parade in Washington.

Some of Sherman's war-hardened units did not cross the Long Bridge into the capital until the morning of May 24. A few hours earlier, 80,000 men of Major General George G. Meade's Army of the Potomac had marched down Pennsylvania Avenue. Now it was time for Sherman's 65,000 veterans—whose bedraggled appearance came from having marched 2,000 miles from Atlanta—to appear before the elite of the nation.

Riding at the head of his troops, Sherman led them past the reviewing stand in which President Johnson, members of his cabinet, and top military officers were seated. As custom dictated, he then dismounted to be seated among the dignitaries.

Observers who trained their field glasses upon the presidential box later said that they saw the man who led the March to the Sea solemnly salute the president. Edwin M. Stanton then extended his hand to shake that of Sherman in a gesture of conciliation.

Earlier, the man from Lancaster had warned, "No man shall insult me with impunity." Having been bushwhacked by politicians, he now acted as though he didn't see the outstretched hand of the secretary of war. In his *Memoirs* the general named for an Indian warrior tersely summarized the dramatic incident by saying, "I do not care to shake hands with clerks."

21

"Women More Dangerous Than Three Companies of Rebels"

"Those Moon women in the Burnet House are more dangerous than three companies of rebels! Keep a sharp eye on them."

"Of course, General Burnside. But wouldn't it be easier to guard them at a more secure place, perhaps Camp Chase?"

"Easier in many respects," confessed the head of the military Department of the Ohio. "But Chase is out of the question. I've known all three for years. Was once very close to them. They are not ordinary prisoners. Keep them under guard at the hotel until I can arrange for a court-martial."

With the question of custody of his prisoners settled, at least for the moment, Major General Ambrose E. Burnside leaned back in his chair, closed his eyes, and laughed aloud. Surprised aides tossed questioning glances at him, but he ignored them and offered no explanation.

Years earlier, when he was not long out of West Point, he had been in Brownsville, Indiana, not far from his birthplace, when two sisters from Ohio came to the village to visit. Little Virginia captivated him when she crawled upon his lap to accept gifts of candy, solemnly surveyed the buttons on his bright uniform, and began to call him Buttons.

But it was Jennie's older sister, Lottie, who won the heart of the artillery officer who delighted in telling stories of how he fought the Apaches in the New Mexico Territory. Witty, vivacious, and beautiful, Lottie was said already to have had more than one sweetheart, but that made no difference to Ambrose. He proposed; she accepted; and they made arrangements to be married.

Indiana native Ambrose E. Burnside is remembered chiefly for having given his name, slightly transformed, to sideburns. [LIBRARY OF CONGRESS]

Tradition says that the wedding ceremony proceeded normally through the point at which the young officer said, "I do." Then the minister posed his question to Lottie Moon, expecting to get an equally firm response. Instead, she giggled, "Not on your life!" and scurried from the room.

Now Lottie, Jennie, and their mother, Cynthia, were his prisoners. He saw no reason to be in a hurry about putting them on trial, and it would be mighty interesting to learn how they came to be such ardent supporters of the rebellion.

Robert Moon, deceased father of Lottie and Jennie, would have been puzzled by their actions. Because he wanted to free the slaves he owned, the Virginia physician bought property in Oxford, Ohio, in 1831. Three years later he took his wife and daughter Lottie to the frontier town, which was especially attractive to him because it contained institutions of higher learning.

A decade after settling close to the winding Talawanda River in the Miami valley, Cynthia Charlotte—known to family and friends as Lottie—was delighted at the birth of a baby sister. Jennie was a charming child but became head-strong and defiant during adolescence.

Enrolled in Oxford Female College, later absorbed by Miami University, she violated rules and was told to behave or leave. Tossing her head defiantly as she left the office of the president, the younger of the Moon sisters went home to get her rifle. Back on campus, she shot a hole in every star of the campus flag. Years later, she laughed that her girlhood exploit was good preparation for her role as a spy for the Confederacy.

Though never sedate, Lottie was more restrained than Jennie. After having left Burnside at the altar and rejecting at least a dozen other suitors, she married James Clark, destined soon to become a judge. They made their home at James Station near Cincinnati, later included in Fairfield. Soon it became a meeting place for people unhappy at the prospect of a war that would pit the North against the South.

Both Clark and his wife were outspokenly in favor of peace at any price, but they did nothing except talk until early 1862 when a one-time military instruction camp at Columbus was fenced with barbed wire and turned into a prison named for the U.S. secretary of the treasury Salmon P. Chase. Constructed to accommodate Southerners captured at Forts Henry and Donelson in Tennessee, Camp Chase was soon reported to hold a prisoner who was special to the Clarks.

At the death of her husband shortly before the outbreak of war, Cynthia Moon and her offspring had moved to Memphis. Despite their Ohio background, her two sons were eager to fight for the Confederacy. William volunteered for the navy, but Robert preferred service on land. Captured, he was reported to have been sent back to Ohio as an inmate of Camp Chase.

As soon as she heard that her brother might be there, Lottie was eager to visit him. Newly elected Governor David Tod, a close friend of her husband, quickly arranged for her to go and come as she wished. However, upon reaching the prison camp, Lottie learned that Bob, an enlisted man, was in another prison as Chase was reserved for captive officers.

Miami University as it appeared when President Hall was condemned for the crime of having been born in the South. [COURTESY UNIVERSITY OF MIAMI]

Taking a quick look about the stockade, she was appalled at the conditions she saw. So she returned again and again, bringing so much food, clothing, and medicine that inmates called her "the Florence Nightingale of Camp Chase." Years later, she said that though she despised the Lincoln administration and hated the war, it was Camp Chase that turned her into an enemy of the Union.

An opportunity to do much more than comfort prisoners soon came her way. Nearby Kentucky, officially neutral and usually labeled a border state, was crucial to both Union and Confederate hopes. General Braxton Bragg set his eyes upon Louisville as a prize, while Major General Kirby Smith considered trying to seize Cincinnati.

By this time, Judge Clark's home had become a regional rendezvous for Copperheads, Peace Democrats who often were more sympathetic with the rebel than with the Union cause. At least as much as any other state and perhaps more, Ohio was politically divided.

Even the Cincinnati *Enquirer* warned readers on May 20, 1862, that abolition of slavery would "ruin the Great Empire of the West" by challenging its monopoly in grain. Pro-

Southern Knights of the Golden Circle could be found throughout the southern part of the state, and they abounded in Butler County. Yet Unionists had such strong feelings that middle-of-the-road President John W. Hall of Miami University was subjected to harassment.

Late in the summer of 1862, Judge Clark and Lottie received a distinguished visitor. Walker Taylor, nephew of former president Zachary Taylor, had on his person secret dispatches for Confederate general Kirby Smith. But he was too well known to attempt to deliver them in Kentucky; would someone volunteer to complete his mission?

Lottie immediately set out for Lexington, crossing the Ohio by way of the Newport ferry. Federal authorities soon learned that a female courier had penetrated their lines, so they doubled their security measures. In this emergency, Lottie disguised herself as a washerwoman for her return home, traveling part of the time, she said, within a few feet of a prominent Union officer.

Emboldened by this success, the woman from Oxford took dispatches to Confederate leaders in Canada without difficulty. Then, disguised as an English invalid, she set out for Richmond to deliver a reply to Jefferson Davis. If her story is to be believed, she somehow persuaded the U.S. secretary of war, Edwin Stanton, to issue her a special pass. Safe from arrest unless her real identity should be discovered, she said that she reached Fredericksburg in the party that included Abraham Lincoln.

Two-way correspondence she carried is believed to have centered upon the Northwestern Conspiracy, an effort by Confederates to bring about a popular uprising against the federal government and the war in Illinois, Indiana, and Ohio. That conspiracy fizzled, and the war wore on. Lottie made a long and dangerous trip to Winchester, Virginia, during which the spy who posed as "an invalid English woman" came under suspicion by Major General Robert Milroy.

Said to have been brought before him for questioning, Lottie resorted to a girlhood trick that had brought many a laugh to her bosom friend, Caroline Scott. Using muscles that few persons ever master, she threw her jaw out of joint as she was ushered into Milroy's presence. Sensitive to harsh sounds made by bone upon bone, the Federal officer concluded that she really was crippled with rheumatism. After a word of sympathy for her affliction, he sent her on her way.

She didn't fare so well when captured in Cincinnati a few months later and brought before Burnside. She started babbling the story that had proved effective in earlier emergencies, but stopped when he waved his hand and said, "You

For post-war dress, Lottie Moon Clark preferred black, reputedly as a sign of mourning for the Lost Cause. [AUTHOR'S COLLECTION]

don't fool me a second, Lottie Moon; you have changed but little since you left me at the altar."

Once she confessed her identity, Lottie got another surprise from Burnside, who told her, "I have two other women in custody here, caught trying to smuggle letters and medicine to the South. Your mother and sister will be glad to see you!"

According to the Cincinnati *Daily Commercial,* the two former residents of Butler County were found with at least twenty-five letters and "a small cargo" on their persons. An inventory showed that the women were transporting to the Confederacy forty bottles of one-eighth-ounce morphine, five balls of opium, a quantity of camphor, and assorted kinds of cloth.

With "the three Moon women" re-united in a guarded hotel room, Ambrose Burnside seems deliberately to have pushed papers aside, if he did not destroy them. Not having arranged for a court-martial after more than three months, he permitted Cynthia, Lottie, and Jennie to be released on their parole, or vow, that they would do nothing to harm the Union cause. Whether or not the three spies kept their promise is uncertain.

At war's end, Lottie and her husband moved to New York City where she became a correspondent for the *World* newspaper. She later spent a time in Paris, covering the Franco-Prussian War. Using the pseudonym Charles M. Clary, Lottie—not related to the Baptist missionary of the same name—wrote several books, the most widely read being *The Modern Hagar.*

When she became seriously ill and took refuge in her son's Philadelphia home, she learned that a girlhood friend still had fond memories of her. At Miami University, the special collections department of the library holds letters written on December 17, 1888, and January 8, 1889. Both are filled with inquiries about the rebel courier whom the writer called Lot Clark. Both are signed by Caroline Scott Harrison, wife of the twenty-third president who spent many weary months on Civil War battlefields fighting against the cause for which Lottie risked her life.

22

Mitchel's Raiders Precipitated an Unequaled Locomotive Chase

"Step forward, young man."

"Yes, sir!" responded Jacob Parrott of Company K, Thirty-third Ohio Infantry Regiment, on March 24, 1863. Conscious of the pounding of his heart, the flush-faced soldier took two brisk steps. Uncertain of what he should do, he tossed a smart salute, then stood at attention.

Wordless, U.S. secretary of war Edwin M. Stanton presented to the Buckeye private the first Congressional Medal of Honor ever bestowed. In turn, five of Parrott's comrades received the most coveted award of the U.S. Army. Survivors of what then was known as Mitchel's Raid, they had reached the capital after an exchange that liberated them from Confederate prisons.

Their saga began as a result of planning by Brigadier General Ormsby Mitchel, who was reared in Lebanon and Xenia. During the Federal campaign against Fort Donelson, Tennessee, Mitchel became acquainted with James J. Andrews. A Virginia native who worked as a house painter, Andrews had moved to Flemingsburg, Kentucky, near the Ohio border and had launched a singing school. When the Civil War started, he offered his services to the Union as a civilian.

Having performed well on a spy mission in which he posed as a quinine dealer, Andrews was told to destroy a railroad bridge over the Tennessee River. He muffed the job, but by the time he rejoined Mitchel near Shelbyville he had developed a new plan.

"The rebels would be helpless without the Western and Atlantic Railroad," he told Mitchel. "This one-track line connects Atlanta with Chattanooga; by cutting it, we would strike a blow at the heart of the Confederacy."

"You propose to burn bridges?"

"First we will steal a locomotive. Heading north, we will burn bridges and tear up track. Not far south of Chattanooga, the railroad runs through a long tunnel. If that should be blown up—and I believe it can—Jefferson Davis will really howl!"

Mitchel listened intently, waved Andrews out of his tent, and sent for his aides. Major General Don Carlos Buell's Army of the Ohio was about to launch a strike against the rebels. If Huntsville, Alabama, could be isolated, the Confederates would be prevented from sending reinforcements from the center. Andrews's plan offered a way to enhance Buell's hopes of a smashing victory.

To accomplish his goal, the bridge-burner would need at least twenty volunteers. Since they must proceed through enemy territory in civilian dress, if captured they would be subject to execution as spies. Did any Ohio unit include men willing to risk their necks?

Colonel Joshua Sill spoke when this decisive question was asked. He knew the men of his brigade "inside and out," he said. If his Buckeyes were offered a chance to strike a decisive blow, the only problem would be selection of men from scores who would want to be involved.

Sill was correct. When the proposed raid was briefly described, so many offered to follow Andrews that it took an hour to select about thirty of the most stalwart volunteers. These men met their leader during the night of April 7 at a farm not far from Shelbyville.

Wearing a Prince Albert coat and a "stovepipe hat" of the sort associated with Abraham Lincoln, Andrews looked every inch the southern gentleman he would pretend to be. He supplied each of his volunteers with Confederate currency, clothing suitable for field work or street wear, and a ball-and-cap revolver.

"Wear your pistol under your coat, at the rear of your belt," Andrews ordered. "Hope not to need it, but be ready to use it in an emergency. Make your way to Marietta, Georgia, in

James J. Andrews, who led the raid and whose name later was attached to it. [AUTHOR'S COLLECTION]

groups of not more than three. Be at this station twenty miles above Atlanta by midnight on Thursday the tenth; this is extremely urgent. We strike early the next morning, and any man who has not appeared will miss his opportunity for glory."

Andrews did not tell his volunteers that their seizure of a locomotive was planned to coincide with the appearance of Mitchel's troops before Huntsville. Even he had no idea that his exploit would become famous as the most dramatic adventure of the Civil War.

Sam Llewellyn and James Smith were only two hours out of Shelbyville before they were stopped and questioned. Following instructions, they said they had come from Fleming County, Kentucky, to volunteer for Confederate service. Taken at their word, both men were promptly enlisted in an artillery battery.

Others were delayed or lost their way in unfamiliar territory; at least two didn't get the wake-up call they had requested from a hotel clerk. As a result the number of raiders was reduced to twenty by the time they were ready to put Andrews's plan into operation.

Only twenty-six-year-old William A. Fuller, conductor of the Western and Atlantic train, was mildly suspicious as men from Ohio piled aboard at Marietta. He had been warned to watch for deserters, and some of these passengers seemed nervous. But the eight-mile trip to Big Shanty was uneventful. By the time they approached it—present-day Kennesaw, Georgia—Fuller was busy walking through cars shouting, "Twenty-minute breakfast stop coming up!"

Fuller and most passengers jumped off the train before it had come to a complete stop and headed for the Lacy Hotel. Private W. J. Knight of the Twenty-first Ohio had experience as a railroad fireman; at a nod from Andrews, he followed his leader out of the passenger car and headed toward the locomotive.

"Good!" grunted Andrews upon finding three empty box cars just behind the engine. These would be perfect for concealing his men from view, and at the proper time their wooden sides and tops could be used to build fast-burning

At intervals the raiders jumped from their locomotive—pulling only one boxcar at the end—to rip up short lengths of track. [AUTHOR'S COLLECTION]

Racing backward, the locomotive Texas approaches a bridge under which raiders had set a fire that failed to burn because of rain. [AUTHOR'S COLLECTION]

fires. At his signal, a raider uncoupled the train between the last box car and the baggage car.

With the cab of the locomotive empty, it was easy for Andrews, Knight, J. A. Wilson, and W. W. Brown to climb into it while their sixteen comrades piled into box cars. As soon as all were aboard, Knight released the brake and pulled hard on the throttle. Chugging forward and rapidly gaining speed, their abbreviated train was on the way to Chattanooga with stops planned only at the Oostanaula River and half a dozen other points that would render the Western and Atlantic impassable. Though authorized by General Ormsby Mitchel and initially designated by his name, the subsequent adventure later came to be known as Andrews's Raid.

When they realized what had happened, conductor William A. Fuller and an aide started an eighty-seven-mile chase after the stolen locomotive on foot. Subsequently they used a pole-pushed handcar, and three separate locomotives commandeered along the way. One of them, the *Texas*, raced backward around sharp curves at top speed for much of the distance.

The story of the race between the Ohio raiders and the Confederate pursuers has been told many times. It was familiar long before Walt Disney used it as the basis for the movie *The Great Locomotive Chase*. Every Civil War buff and

J. A. Wilson of the 21st Ohio spoke from the scaffold before the mass execution of seven raiders in Atlanta. [AUTHOR'S COLLECTION]

many members of the general population know that eventually Andrews ran out of fuel and had to abandon the stolen locomotive. Damage to the Western and Atlantic was limited to tearing up a few rails and cutting telegraph lines. Bridges proved too wet to burn and the all-important tunnel was not damaged.

Andrews's men scattered into nearby woods when the stolen locomotive came to a halt, but most of them were soon captured. Hasty trials pronounced the raiders to be spies who were disguised as civilians; so punishment was swift and decisive. Andrews was hanged in Atlanta on June 7; eleven days later, seven of his followers were escorted to a mass gallows.

Knowing their lives to be worthless, fourteen raiders broke out of the Atlanta jail and divided into pairs. Eight men managed to elude pursuers and most of these eventually fought under Ohio-born General William Rosecrans at Chickamauga and Missionary Ridge. Three pairs were quickly recaptured; after weeks of imprisonment they were central to a mass exchange that brought them to Washington to receive the Congressional Medals of Honor.

Long after the first six medals were conferred upon the valiant Buckeye soldiers, awards were made to their comrades, some posthumously. Merited as were the awards, said James B. Fry, the entire episode called for after-the-fact evaluation. Having been chief of staff to Buell when the Mitchel raid was authorized, he admitted that he had encouraged it.

Viewing it from the perspective of two decades and judging its military rather than its melodramatic value, the brigadier general reached a solemn conclusion. "Mitchel's bridge-burners," said Fry, "took desperate chances to accomplish objects of no substantial advantage."

23

Billy Quantrill's Turn-about Life Ended in a Louisville Jail

"Got us another 'un locked in my smokehouse."

"Where'd he come from, Frank?"

"Stopped at my place and asked how to find the home of Jim Lane. That a dead giveaway, so I told him he needed something to eat. Set him down at the table—never saw a fellow so hungry—and hit him in the back of the head with an ax handle."

"Don't know what we'd do without an enterprising fellow like you, Frank," commented an Ohio native who had recently joined a gang of jayhawkers operating near the ferry landing at Lawrence, Kansas. "What do you figure this one is worth?"

"Has nearly all his teeth and a good set of muscles. He's maybe twenty-five years old; ought to bring four hundred dollars, maybe more."

"Sounds mighty good. When do we move?" inquired William Clarke Quantrill, known to intimates as Billy.

"Not tonight. Somebody could have seen him crossing the river. Moon ought to be right about Friday. By then, he'll tell us where he came from, or we'll beat it out of him."

With their plans matured, the band of border ruffians that included Frank Baldwin, Quantrill, Jake Herd, and Esau Jager waited impatiently. Friday night they crossed the nearby border into Missouri, where they soon found the owner of the fugitive who had expected to find freedom in Kansas. Jake, an expert at haggling, was delegated to do the talking. Before he nodded to comrades that their captive should be delivered, he casually pocketed five hundred dollars in gold that he divided with his comrades.

Strife-filled Lawrence, Kansas, was far different from peaceful Canal Dover, Ohio, where Billy was born in 1837. His father, a tinsmith, and mother soon regretted that they had not named him for his uncle Jesse, a professional forger and con man whom he strongly resembled.

"Acts just like Jesse, too," his mother commented one day when the boy was about fourteen. "Sally Tompkins was at the mill this morning. Told me she'd seen that boy running through the woods, wasting good ammunition by shootin' squirrels and rabbits for the fun of it. Didn't even bother to pick 'em up and bring 'em home with him."

If the young marksman actually had the wild streak his parents believed they saw in him, it did not show up at school. He learned so easily that at sixteen, a year before his father died of consumption, he became a teacher in the Canal Dover school.

When the death of Tom Quantrill left the family destitute, his widow began taking in boarders. Billy said he didn't like the idea of being dependent on them, so he decided to go west to try his luck. Not finding life there any easier than in Ohio, he wound up teaching school in Mendota, Illinois, and Fort Wayne, Indiana.

At first his monthly salary of twenty dollars, on top of board and lodging, sounded mighty good to him. Soon, however, he found the long school day to be so tiresome that he drifted back to Canal Dover, where the only work he could find was at the familiar little school house. The allegiances of his older students reflected those of their parents; some talked eagerly of a war to free the slaves, but others stoutly insisted, "A slave is property, and a fellow has the right to defend anything he has ever bought."

Not simply in rural Ohio but throughout the nation, it was generally understood that Kansas might turn the tide in Congress when the territory became a state. If settlers decided in favor of slavery there, the delicate balance in the U.S. Senate would be tipped in favor of the South. Therefore, hoping to

A typical band of the border ruffians who caused Kansas to be universally known as "bleeding." [YALE UNIVERSITY ART GALLERY]

determine the outcome of the struggle in Kansas, wagon trains set out from Atlanta and other southern cities.

Once abolitionists learned about the increased flow of immigrants from the South, they got busy. In New England the brother of Harriet Beecher Stowe organized a society whose goal was to send enough settlers to Kansas to guarantee that voters would reject slavery in the territory. Many a Kansas-bound immigrant carried with him what he called "one of Beecher's Bibles," a Sharp's rifle provided by the most prominent clergyman in the nation.

Badly divided in sentiment, Ohio included numerous men who said they hated slavery and who welcomed a chance to go west and make their fortunes. In 1837 these abolitionists made up several Kansas-bound wagon trains. One of them snaked into Canal Dover and paused overnight. Early the next morning they picked up Colonel Henry Torry, Harmon V. Beeson with his son Richard, and a weary young teacher who had already chosen the name he planned to use in Kansas: Charley Hart.

Once they reached the plains state, Hart cut loose from his Ohio connection in spite of his promise to work for Beeson long enough to pay for the trip. Calling himself a detective who was being paid by the Delaware Indians, he drifted into Lawrence and decided to stay.

Soon he joined a band of locals who were ardent admirers of "Captain" John Stewart, a well-established jayhawker. Charley followed Stewart on several raids into proslavery Missouri and gradually made friends with the band that looked to Frank Baldwin for leadership. Still calling himself a detective, he proved that he could shoot an unarmed villager as casually as he had downed a rabbit or a squirrel in boyhood.

Many an analyst has pondered the riddle: How did a peaceful young schoolteacher from an abolitionist family become a notorious leader of those who plundered antislavery settlers in Kansas?

Everything in the record suggests that the answer to that question is simple. Quantrill was intelligent, but lazy. He wanted money—lots of money—the easiest way he could get it. In Kansas he could loaf all day most days, so long as he could at intervals share in the ransom for a kidnapped black or in the plunder from a defenseless settlement or mail coach. Writing home, he pretended that John Brown's murders "made a Southerner out of him." Actually he was almost as ready to prey upon proslavery settlers as upon abolitionists.

During a brief informal connection with a Confederate military unit, he was on hand for a fierce battle at Wilson's Creek. Even though given a commission as a captain, he quickly tired of military life, returned to Kansas, and formed his own band of bushwhackers. Quantrill's men became so notorious that early in 1862 Federal authorities branded them as outlaws.

Instead of going into hiding, Quantrill and his men increased the pace of their attacks, claiming to strike at Union sympathizers but actually hitting farmers regardless of their views. On August 21, 1863, the man from Ohio rode into Lawrence, Kansas, at the head of a force that had grown to

RUINS OF LAWRENCE, KANSAS.

When Quantrill's raiders turned their backs upon the center of Lawrence, they left behind only smoldering ruins that concealed the bodies of many dead civilians. [FRANK LESLIE'S ILLUSTRATED WEEKLY]

about 450 men. They fanned out through the growing town, killing those who resisted before plundering stores and hotels, then turning to private homes. Once a building had been emptied of valuables and supplies, it was burned.

No one knows how many civilians died in the Lawrence massacre, the worst of its sort during the war. At least 150 men, women, and children were killed; the number may have reached 200.

By now described by one of his own lieutenants as "intoxicated by the blood of his victims," Quantrill surprised and overwhelmed a body of about fifty Federals at Baxter Springs. Among those who surrendered without serious resistance were at least seventeen civilians, most of them musicians. All of them, including a boy of twelve, were butchered before the wagons containing their bodies were burned. Soldiers were held as prisoners, perhaps with the hope that authorities would pay a generous ransom for their release.

With a price on his head and his name plastered across

wanted posters in nearly every village and town of Kansas, the man who still sometimes demanded to be addressed as Charley Hart, detective of the Delaware Indians, turned back toward the east. Leading about thirty followers into Kentucky, he pillaged, robbed, and killed with abandon until ambushed by a small force of Federal irregulars near Taylorsville. Seriously wounded, he was taken to Louisville for medical treatment designed to prepare him for the hangman.

William Clarke Quantrill cheated justice once more. His condition gradually deteriorated so much that no one would agree to serve as his executioner. At age forty-one, the one-time schoolteacher from Canal Dover who was the most brutal partisan leader of the Civil War died in his cell. Always Charley Hart had been careful to stay away from photographers and artists, so likenesses of him are rare. During his last hours, in periods of delirium he sometimes mumbled as though talking to unruly students. But if he was troubled by memories of his atrocities, he kept such thoughts to himself even on his deathbed.

PART FIVE:
Mavericks, Strays, and Zealots

Brigham Young, who spent formative years in Ohio, would easily win in a contest for the title of "most married American." His enthusiasm for the cause of Latter-day Saints was engendered in part, harsh critics said, by their endorsement of polygamy.

Wilbur and Orville Wright would be unknown had they not had such zeal that some who knew them well called them fanatics. In the eyes of Abraham Lincoln, the leader of Democrats in Ohio was much more than a maverick; Vallandigham was downright dangerous. Victoria Woodhull's zeal may have stemmed from a mixture of greed and credulity.

Ohioans have always included a wonderfully diverse mixture of people, both native born and newcomers.

Pontiac's siege of fort Detroit, as depicted by Frederick Remington.
[*Harper's Encyclopedia of U.S. History* (1905)]

24

The Name of Pontiac Is Alive Today

Major Henry Gladwin believed that trouble was brewing, so he took extraordinary safety measures. As the officer in charge of Fort Detroit, he well knew its history and vulnerability. It had been established in 1701 by the French as Fort Pontchartrain and became an important trading post. During the conflict later known as the French and Indian War, the British gained control of it in 1760. However, throughout the region many Indians were French allies and would like nothing better than to brandish a scalp taken from a slain Redcoat.

Matters reached a crisis in May 1763. A tall and stalwart young Ottawa chieftain, wearing a stone in his nose and beads in his ears, bowed respectfully and signaled that he wished to enter the fort. Silver trade bracelets that dangled on his forearms seemed to proclaim that he had been in frequent contact with white settlers along the Detroit River.

Gesturing, Gladwin indicated that the visitor and his sixty-warrior entourage could enter the compound whose circular wall of cedar pickets was fifteen feet high and stretched for nearly 1,200 yards. No one needed to tell the English officer, a veteran of many battles, who was leading the ceremonial party. No doubt about it, the man was Pontiac, called "Emperor of the Natives" by some settlers. Known as a persuasive orator and a cunning strategist, Pontiac was up to no good, the major sensed, in spite of his seeming to want a peaceful parley.

Once inside the fenced area, the Ottawas and Hurons who made up the party of visitors moved into a rhythmic ceremonial dance. Meanwhile, each warrior tried to select the

Redcoat or defensive position he would attack upon a signal from his leader. All who followed Pontiac had seen his wampum belt, green on one side and white on the other, that he planned to present to Gladwin. It was to be proffered with the white side up; when turned by Pontiac to reveal the green, every man who followed him was to move into swift action.

However, the leader of the tribesmen quickly sensed that the Redcoats were not duped, that they were ready for whatever might take place. Every sentry was at his post; no soldier was seen sprawling in the shade with his musket lying at his feet. To attack as planned would bring diaster, Pontiac decided. When he solemnly presented the wampum belt, white side up, he did not suspect that an Indian woman whom Gladwin had taken as his lover might have warned him of the impending attack.

Thus Pontiac and his warriors left the compound without incident and retired to the spot where their sixty-five canoes were beached. Half a dozen cannon manned by the defenders meant that an all-out frontal assault upon Fort Detroit would be suicidal. Hence the band of Indians from several tribes crawled into position behind logs and launched a siege. No one, neither defenders or attackers, then could predict that the stand-off would last until November. But everyone believed that it might signal the start of a long-expected Indian uprising aimed at driving the British from the region of the Great Lakes.

No one was better prepared to lead this venture than the warrior known to white settlers as Ponteach, or Pontiac. He had been born about 1720 in a Maumee River village not far from present-day Toledo. One of his parents was an Ottawa and the other a Chippewa (properly known as Ojibwa). A skilled organizer, he became leader of the united bands of Chippewa, Potawatomi, and Ottawa Indians. Later this coalition included almost all of the tribes in the entire Mississippi Valley. Friendly toward the British at first, he had switched allegiance to the French in 1760 after it became apparent English settlers would encroach upon the Indians' ancestral lands. French hunters and traders encouraged him with vague promises of help from France.

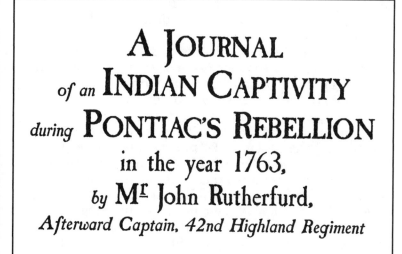

A JOURNAL
of an INDIAN CAPTIVITY
during PONTIAC'S REBELLION
in the year 1763,
by Mr John Rutherfurd,
Afterward Captain, 42nd Highland Regiment

Title page of a diary kept by prisoner John Rutherfurd, who was age seventeen at the time of his capture. [NEW YORK PUBLIC LIBRARY]

The siege of Detroit was abandoned because the Indians were unaccustomed to this type of warfare and some tribes disaffected in what has become known in American history as Pontiac's War. Almost simultaneously, his warriors moved toward every British fort west of the mountains. They swarmed upon Sandusky, quickly overpowering its defenders and killing all fifteen men who made up the garrison.

Sir Jeffrey Amherst, British commander in chief in America, was contemptuous of the Indians and their French allies. He had driven them from Lake Champlain in 1759 as a prelude to capturing Montreal in 1760, when all Canada fell to the British and he became governor general. So he was furious when he learned that a fresh batch of trouble had been brewed by "the vilest race of creatures on the face of the earth."

Amherst correctly concluded that Pontiac was "the chief ringleader of mischief," so he offered a reward of 100 pounds to anyone who would kill him. "Take no prisoners," he instructed his subordinates; "put to death all Indians that fall into your hands."

Unaware that Sir Jeffrey had issued a public proclamation calling for his assassination, Pontiac sent bands of warriors against ten other British forts. All but four were captured, with most of the garrisons wiped out. Frontier settlements were plundered and laid desolate.

Some British reinforcements were annihilated. Only occasionally did the Indians take prisoners when defenses collapsed. Young John Rutherfurd kept a detailed diary during his captivity and reported that by the end of July men led by Pontiac held more than fifty Englishmen. Peering from a window, he saw eight of them murdered in a single day. Skin was pulled from arms of the dead, said Rutherfurd, "to make tobacco pouches of, leaving the first joints of the fingers by way of tassels."

The larger struggle between England and France, known as the Seven Years War in Europe, ended in 1763, and by 1764 continuing British action against France's Indian allies in North America began to take its toll. Pontiac could no longer arouse his confederation of tribes to continue to fight what was obviously a lost cause. He made peace in July 1766. His stand against encroachment on Indian territory was over. He returned to his home in what is now the state of Ohio.

Three years later Pontiac visited Cahokia, a village in the vicinity of St. Louis. There the architect of the most powerful of all American Indian confederations died at about age forty-five, the victim not of a Redcoat's bullet but of the knife of a fellow tribesman believed to have been bribed by a white man.

Nevertheless, Pontiac's memory is alive today in the land he loved. Not only is his war detailed in all history books of the period, three American cities memorialize his name. What begun as Pontiac Spring Wagon Works is now General Motors, whose Pontiac cars traverse the nation's highways.

25

Master Perry Requested Dangerous Duty—And Got It

"You have come about the situation on Lake Erie?"

"Yes, your excellency, I would give everything I have for a chance to settle things there."

Governor William Jones of Rhode Island leaned forward, punctuating his words with a pointing forefinger: "I quite understand, Master Perry. You'd like to redeem yourself for the wreck of the *Revenge*."

"Of course. But since a court of inquiry has cleared me, that is secondary. Most of all, I want to serve my country—and to rid our Great Lakes of the British."

Master Commandant Oliver Perry rose to his full five feet, six inches and pounded his open left hand with his right fist. "It is common knowledge that Commodore Chauncey has entered a plea for help. Scuttlebutt has it that President Madison himself is greatly concerned over our inability to continue commerce on the lakes."

"You are correct, sir. Still, you are young and have had limited combat experience. This calls for a seasoned veteran; it may well be the most dangerous assignment now open."

"Wonderful! Perhaps you do not know my full name, Your Excellency. My parents called me Oliver Hazard Perry, and that middle name is symbolic. I am ready to go; please let me."

"I will forward your request to Isaac Chauncey, now somewhere on Lake Ontario. If he approves, this new tour of duty is yours, sir."

*   *   *

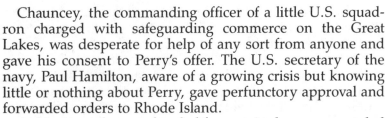

*Oliver H. Perry, recently
promoted to a grade halfway
between that of lieutenant
and captain, began his naval
service as a midshipman at
age fourteen.* [HARPER'S
ENCYCLOPEDIA OF U.S.
HISTORY (1908)]

Chauncey, the commanding officer of a little U.S. squadron charged with safeguarding commerce on the Great
Lakes, was desperate for help of any sort from anyone and
gave his consent to Perry's offer. The U.S. secretary of the
navy, Paul Hamilton, aware of a growing crisis but knowing
little or nothing about Perry, gave perfunctory approval and
forwarded orders to Rhode Island.

At Newport the man headed for certain danger persuaded
many of the men aboard his gunboats to go with him, then
turned over command of the little flotilla to a subordinate.
Following instructions of Chauncey, the party set out for
Albany on February 17, 1813. From that city they proceeded
to Sacket's Harbor, New York, by sleigh.

In March Perry was at Presque Isle, Pennsylvania (now
Erie), in search of ships. Though local builders were willing
to go to work, he judged their number inadequate. So he
went to Black Rock, near Buffalo, where he found Scottish-
born ship builder Henry Eckford eager to help drive British
warships from America's inland waters.

Late in April five merchant vessels, hastily converted into

naval craft by Eckford, joined the four tiny warships under construction on Cascade Creek near Erie. By July 10 Perry's little fleet was ready for action. His flagship, the *Lawrence,* was named in honor of Captain James Lawrence, who had died in a vain attempt on June 1 to capture the British frigate *Shannon.*

In a council of war with General William Henry Harrison, commander of all forces in the Northwest, Perry requested and received permission to move to a base he considered more suitable. Thus at Put-in-Bay near Sandusky something new arrived on Lake Erie: ten small U.S. warships armed with cannon that seemed almost like toys in comparison with those on British vessels.

Perry established a lookout post on a nearby island but gained no vital information after days of observation. Frustrated, he began cruising about the lake in an attempt to find

As he lay dying five days after having failed to defeat a British warship, Capt. James Lawrence reputedly uttered words that formed Perry's banner. [HARPER'S ENCYCLOPEDIA OF U.S. HISTORY (1908)]

the enemy. Success came on September 10, when the look-out in the main-top of the *Lawrence* shouted, "Sail ho!"

Sailing briskly toward the British squadron barely visible on the horizon, Perry broke out and hoisted a square flag his men had never seen. White embroidered letters against a blue background proclaimed Don't Give Up the Ship, an abbreviated version of the final order of the mortally wounded Captain James Lawrence. Unaware that the approaching vessels were commanded by Robert H. Barclay, who had fought with Nelson at Trafalgar, Perry's men gave three hearty cheers in honor of the vivid new emblem floating from the main yard.

The opposing forces joined battle at noon. Though the British squadron included only eight vessels, their armament was much heavier and their gunners were combat veterans. Barclay, shrewdly directing much of his fire at the *Lawrence,* quickly cut her sails into ribbons and then disabled most of her twenty guns by direct hits. A seaman who cried, "We have become a sitting duck!" was ordered below and put into irons. "We fight to the finish!" Perry shouted above the roar of enemy guns.

Realizing that the *Lawrence* would soon sink, the youthful commander signaled for his banner to be lowered. Yanking it from ropes, he wrapped it around his body and took to a rowboat to try to reach the nearby *Niagara.* When he asked for volunteer oarsmen, every able-bodied man aboard the *Lawrence* stepped forward. Selecting four, Perry set out for the *Niagara.*

During fifteen dreadful minutes, the rowboat was under constant fire from big guns whose projectiles often splashed columns of water over the oarsmen but never scored a hit. Signaling for his blue banner to be raised again, Perry sent the *Niagara* directly into the fire of Barclay's *Detroit.*

Having been seriously wounded an hour earlier, the British commander struck his colors less than ten minutes after Perry turned the *Niagara* toward him. Five other British officers followed Barclay's example, but men aboard two small vessels turned and fled. Pursued by Perry's little *Scorpion,* they were overtaken and captured late in the afternoon.

Hastily scrawled, Perry's message about victory on Lake Erie has inspired generations of U.S. naval officers and men. [HARPER'S ENCYCLOPEDIA OF U.S. HISTORY (1908)]

Only when victory was made secure by the sight of three ships headed toward Put-in-Bay by moonlight did Oliver Hazard Perry pause to send a message to Harrison. With his naval cap lying upon his knee, he held an old letter upon its stiff top. Using the stub of a pencil, he wrote a brief report that ended, "We have met the enemy, and they are ours: two ships, two brigs, one schooner, and one sloop."

Destined to become immortal, this terse summary meant that British naval supremacy on the Great Lakes had come to an end. Supplies and men could now pour into Cleveland and other ports to boost the strength of William Henry Harrison's army.

Perry had requested and gotten dangerous duty that led to a stunning victory. Recognizing that the naval encounter was a turning point in the war with Britain, President James Madison promoted the young hero to the rank of captain. In January 1814 Congress gave official thanks to the winner of the Lake Erie battle and ordered a special gold medal to be struck in his honor.

Obverse and reverse of the Perry Medal ordered by Congress—and made of solid gold. [NATIONAL ARCHIVES]

Not until months later did the man who prided himself upon being named Hazard learn the full extent of his victory. Fighting on inland waters at age twenty-eight, Perry had become the first commander ever to force surrender of a squadron of British warships, pride of a nation whose boast was "Britannia Rules the Waves."

Note: Lawrence's last words, shortened by Perry for his battle flag, were: "Tell the men to fire faster and not to give up the ship." Perry's flag inscribed with his version of the order now hangs in Memorial Hall at the U.S. Naval Academy at Annapolis.

26

God Began Whispering to John Brown As an Adolescent in Hudson

John Brown was working for a rich man, but had mighty little himself. When Simon Perkins decided to set up a wool depot in Massachusetts, he told John he'd have to go there and take charge of it.

John's eighty-acre place in Hudson township had been put up for auction at a sheriff's sale, and a fellow named Amos Chamberlain had bought it.

When John heard about what had happened, he said the wool business up East would have to wait. Almighty God had told him that the place belonged to him, and nobody else. So he and two of his boys got their guns and headed for Hudson. The only log cabin on the place was deserted, so John cut a few holes in the wall and turned it into a fort. Said he'd die before he would give it up to Chamberlain or anybody else.

That started a standoff that lasted until food and water ran out. Brown finally gave up to the law and didn't even try to make bail. He was hauled off to the lockup, where he tried to file a lawsuit against Chamberlain for trespassing. When nobody was willing to appear against him, the sheriff finally turned him loose.

Nearly everybody already thought the fellow was a mite touched in the head; they said it was because his mother's brother and sister both went crazy. But until he took the law into his own hands over a worn-out piece of land, nobody thought John Brown might be dangerous.

Transmitted orally for generations and still current in rural areas of Ohio, that story points to what may have been the first act of violence on the part of a crusader whom some admirers have called "God's angry man." Only a few years later, having settled in Osawatomie, Kansas, and trying to hold the territory against slave holders, Brown heard that

When photographed in Akron in 1855, John Brown had not yet begun to grow the beard that was briefly his trademark. [AUTHOR'S COLLECTION]

pro-Southerners had killed political opponents in Lawrence. Settlers who wanted slavery went on a rampage in the free-soil town. Before they quit burning and looting, a few abolitionists were lying on the ground, dead.

Leading four of his sons and two other men, John Brown set out to get revenge and teach slave holders a lesson they'd never forget. During the night of May 23, 1856, they hit homes of settlers along Pottawatomie Creek. Without bothering to find how these strangers stood on the slavery issue, the band of avengers hacked men and women to death with long-edged swords.

Just three years later, Brown and twenty-one followers captured the U.S. Arsenal at Harpers Ferry, Virginia, and held it until they were overcome by marines led by Lieutenant Colonel Robert E. Lee. When a hasty trial led to Brown's execution for treason against the state of Virginia, he became internationally renowned as a martyr of the antislavery movement.

Settlers around Hudson, Ohio, in 1805 didn't find anything unusual about the five-year-old boy, except his tale of having walked most of the way from Connecticut. Questioned, he said that some days he stayed in the saddle from sunup to sundown, herding the family cows. According to the boy's father, Owen, the trip had taken forty-eight days, with his wife and baby riding in an ox-drawn wagon.

They pushed through New York and Pennsylvania to reach New Connecticut and the half-finished cabin that Owen had started a year earlier. Like many others who headed to the region from the East, they were drawn by the lure of cheap land.

John remembered little about his early childhood except "having been thoroughly whipped" by his mother for stealing three brass pins. Once at their new home, the boy whimpered at night for fear that Indians would attack, "but this soon wore off." By age six he had learned to dress the skins of deer, squirrels, and raccoons. Somehow he acquired a yellow marble, unlike any he had ever seen, and he cried for days after losing it.

During warm months he wore nothing except a pair of buckskin breeches suspended by a single shoulder strap. At age eight when he learned that his mother was dead, he sobbed almost as hard as he had when a pet squirrel escaped. When his father took Sally Root as his second wife, John formed an instant dislike for her. Once when she climbed into a hay loft in search of eggs, the nine-year-old tripped her. Badly bruised by her fall, she never quite forgave her stepson.

During the War of 1812 the growing boy helped his father to round up wild stray cattle, then herded them one hundred miles or more to army posts in Michigan. On one of these cattle drives, John found lodging for a night with a landlord who owned a slave about his age. The curiosity of the strange-looking boy turned to fury against the landlord when John saw him beat the young slave with a fire shovel because he had chopped wood too slowly.

During his years in Kansas, Brown said that it was the beating of the boy with an iron implement that had made him an undying foe of slavery. Turned off by what he saw of military life, he decided to "pay fines like a Quaker" so he wouldn't have to join the militia and take part in drills and exercises.

At age sixteen John joined the Congregational church and started studying for the ministry because he heard God calling him. He attended schools in Massachusetts and Connecticut but soon found that reading caused him to become dizzy. Back in Hudson, he resumed work as a tanner and sometimes helped his brother Salmon cut big logs for the ten-foot fireplace.

Many nights their father sat before the fire with two of the younger children in his arms. Owen told them stories of his own childhood and often led the family in singing their favorite song, "Blow Ye the Trumpet, Blow."

At age twenty John married Dianthe Lusk. Twelve years and seven children later, she was dead. After observing "a proper period of grieving" for eleven months, the widower chose a second wife who was thirteen years his junior. Obedient to biblical injunctions concerning fertility, she presented her husband with one baby after another. Eventually he called himself "the proud father of twenty."

Before reaching half that total, Brown became a wanderer. He moved in and out of Ohio and from town to town within the state at least ten times during twenty years. Always hoping to strike it rich but never succeeding, he worked with

At Harpers Ferry, U.S. Marines used a ladder as a battering ram to break down the door that shielded Brown's "army of the Lord." [FRANK LESLIE'S ILLUSTRATED WEEKLY]

John Brown's last written words, scribbled while he waited to go to his death as a traitor to Virginia. [VIRGINIA STATE LIBRARY]

half a dozen partners and backers. He built a tannery at Hudson, surveyed land for Oberlin College, experimented with silk, tried his hand as a developer of land at Franklin Mills (now Kent), then produced and bought wool.

Simon Perkins, son of the co-founder of Akron, provided the bankroll for Brown's most ambitious business venture. Having developed skill in judging the quality and value of wool, he set out to corner the market. This enterprise took him to England in an effort to get high prices but cost Perkins an estimated $40,000 when the bubble burst.

By age fifty John Brown had wandered in and out of a dozen localities and had failed in half a dozen different ventures. Then wealthy Gerrit Smith, the New Yorker who gave Oberlin College the raw land Brown surveyed, took the wandering failure under his wing. Soon he was headed for Kansas on behalf of the Emigration Society, which hoped to attract enough abolitionists to keep the territory free of slavery.

By this time, the man who grew up in Hudson and spent his most promising years in Akron had recruited Edwin Coppock of Salem and other followers in addition to his sons and sons-in-law. With them, John Brown formed his "army of the Lord" and went to Virginia to launch a new nation peopled with former slaves.

Brown remained calm and poised while the hangman made final preparations. [VIRGINIA STATE LIBRARY]

He was surprised and disappointed at failing to attract masses of black followers, yet he persisted in his goal of carving a new nation from the United States. To get weapons stored at Harpers Ferry, he stormed the arsenal and briefly held it against all comers.

His death on the gallows provided John Brown with his only success, turning him into a martyr for his cause. While waiting to be hanged in Charles Town, Virginia, on December 2, 1857, he handed one of his guards a slip of paper on which he had written a terse summary that proved to be prophetic: "I, John Brown, am now quite *certain* that the crimes of this *guilty land will* never be purged away, but with Blood. I had, *as I now think, vainly* flattered myself that without *very much* bloodshed it might be done."

Just two years later, South Carolina voted to secede and one Cotton Belt state after another followed. With Abraham Lincoln waiting to be inaugurated, the Civil War that cost the lives of 623,000 American fighting men became inevitable.

A memorial to John Brown was dedicated in Akron's Perkins Woods in 1938; thirty-three years later, his Akron cottage was refurbished. An elaborate monument to his follower Edwin Coppock stands in Salem.

27

U. S. Grant's Doggedness Brought Him a Smashing Victory

Twisting slowly in the breeze, a piece of paper drifted from a fifth- or sixth-story window of one of New York's tallest buildings. A pedestrian noticed it but continued walking briskly. Suddenly a gust brought it directly in front of him, about five feet from the sidewalk. Instinctively, he reached out and caught the fluttering fragment of newspaper.

Headlines two columns wide proclaimed, "Grant Reported to Be Facing Bankruptcy." Smaller type reported that the brokerage firm of Grant and Ward had lost money heavily, forcing the former president to borrow from William H. Vanderbilt in order to continue in business. Now falling prices meant the firm must be dissolved, leaving the man who had led the Union armies to victory deeply in debt.

The tradition is that chance having informed Mark Twain of Grant's personal crisis, the humorist proposed a novel solution. "Write your memoirs in full; write for the common man," he urged. "That's something no former president has done. Tell the colorful story of your action-filled life as only you can do. Then turn the manuscript over to me. I will publish it, and the proceeds will wipe out your debt, perhaps yield enough to provide you with a few comforts as you grow old."

Whatever the exact circumstances that brought Grant and Twain together, the two agreed upon a course of action. Grant would start putting his experiences upon paper and Twain would organize bands of salesmen to take the published memoirs to the American public. Both of them were

Lt. Gen. Ulysses S. Grant, supreme commander of U.S. forces during the closing months of the Civil War. [NATIONAL ARCHIVES]

keenly aware of two major problems: Grant had written nothing except a few articles for *Century* magazine, and Twain had never been the publisher of a book.

His desperation forced the ex-president into a task he did not relish and for which he felt inadequate. Therefore he turned to Adam Badeau, one of his former military secretaries, and asked for help. Eager to get started, Badeau wanted what his former commander could not give, a salary of $1,000 a month in advance.

Believing himself still feeling the effects of a nasty fall and not yet aware that he had a terminal case of cancer, Ulysses S. Grant decided to tell the story of his life without the assistance of a ghost writer. Retiring to a country home in Mount McGregor, New York, he hired a stenographer and started to work.

The death of his grandmother, the new author began, caused the family of Captain Noah Grant to break up. One of the boys, Jesse, was taken into the home of Judge Tod whose son David became governor of Ohio in 1862. "I was born on the twenty-seventh of April 1822, at Point Pleasant, Clermont County, Ohio," Jesse's son told his secretary. "In the fall of 1823 we moved to Georgetown, the county seat of Brown, the adjoining county east. This place remained my home, until at the age of seventeen, in 1839, I went to West Point."

Often pausing to gather his thoughts before resuming dictation, Grant vividly remembered: "A military life had no charms for me, and I had not the faintest idea of staying in the army even if I should be graduated, which I did not expect."

Upon arrival at the academy the young man who had been baptized Hiram Ulysses and whose education was limited to "subscription schools" was asked his name. Apprehensive that the initials HUG would embarrass him, he responded vigorously, "Ulysses Hiram Grant." He was surprised that the clerk who questioned him shook his head in bewilderment, but he thought little of the incident at the moment.

Soon he learned that Senator Thomas Morris, who was responsible for his appointment, had listed him as Ulysses

Simpson Grant. That name had already gone into the records; perhaps they could be corrected, but it would take time and effort to do so. In a spur of the moment decision, the cadet shrugged his shoulders and decided to keep the name bestowed upon him by mistake.

His academic record was only passable, but his fellow cadets admired him as a superb horseman and a better than average artist. Assigned to the Fourth Infantry upon graduation, his first eleven years in uniform were undistinguished. Shunted from one desolate and isolated post to another, the man now married to the former Julia Dent but usually separated from her was persuaded to submit his resignation.

He regretted having to take off his uniform but welcomed the return to civilian life. During six years he tried a variety of vocations but succeeded at nothing—farming, real estate sales, clerkship in a customs office. In desperation, he worked briefly for his brothers-in-law in Galena, Illinois, and tried to sell firewood in St. Louis. William T. Sherman, who had come to the city to superintend a street railway, saw his shabby former comrade on the streets and was overcome with pity.

Having failed in both military and civilian life, Grant left Galena, Illinois, to take command of a regiment of militia. [AUTHOR'S COLLECTION]

Outbreak of the Civil War seemed to offer Grant a chance to make a new start, so he took his record to the Cincinnati headquarters of General George B. McClellan and asked for an interview. Ignored for two full days, he gave up and returned to Galena. Since governors were authorized to appoint militia officers, Richard Yates of Illinois made him colonel of the state's Twenty-first Volunteer Regiment.

To the surprise of many who had known him earlier, it was Grant—already a brigadier general—who scored the first significant Federal victory of the war at Fort Donelson, Tennessee. Playing upon the initials to which he had become accustomed, he demanded "Unconditional Surrender" of the installation. When he got it, the man who grew up in Georgetown became an instant hero. Admirers showered him with thousands of cigars—now considered to have contributed to the development of his cancer of the mouth and throat.

Abraham Lincoln admired him "because he will fight," and on Lincoln's nomination he became the first lieutenant general of the U.S. Army since George Washington. Unsparing in his use of overwhelming manpower, he relentlessly

Grant's autobiography, the first of its kind, was finished after he was no longer able to dictate to a stenographer. [LIBRARY OF CONGRESS]

Three days before his death, Grant suddenly became strong enough to read a newspaper on the porch of his Mount McGregor home. [GRANT COTTAGE STATE HISTORICAL SITE (NEW YORK)]

pushed Confederate forces to the point of exhaustion and surrender. His military victories having paved the way, he went on to the White House.

Already at a serious stage when he reached agreement with Mark Twain, the ex-president's throat deteriorated rapidly. Eventually he was unable to speak clearly, but he was within perhaps one hundred pages of being through with his life story.

Weary beyond anything he had experienced during years of constant fighting and so weak that he found it difficult to stand, Grant was obsessed with "arriving at honorable settlement of all debts." So he dismissed his secretary and began painfully to write with pen and ink.

To those intimates who remained with him, the dying man wrote: "A verb is anything that signifies to be; to do; or to suffer. I must be a verb; I signify all three." Covered with blankets and shawls and scribbling on oversize sheets of paper with a pencil, he resorted to morphine in order to continue his writing. Only days before his death on July 23, 1885, U. S. Grant completed the voluminous story of his life, filled with heartbreaking failures but also triumphant successes.

Mark Twain, meanwhile, had contracted with a printing house with a record of having turned out well-produced

Established publishers ridiculed Mark Twain as "riding his jumping frog toward disaster" with the Grant memoirs. [NEW YORK PUBLIC LIBRARY]

books. He advertised for "canvassers" in newspapers of major eastern cities, recruited great numbers of them, and set out personally to train them. Each salesman was presented with a copy of Twain's pamphlet titled "How to Introduce the Personal Memoirs of U. S. Grant." By the time two handsome green and gold volumes came from the press, the famous humorist had about ten thousand men ready to canvass the nation door to door.

U. S. Grant's *Memoirs*, the first presidential autobiography written for the general public with the hope of making a substantial profit, proved to be a smashing success. With the annual salary of the president of the United States pegged at $50,000, Twain's first check to the Grant estate was in the amount of $250,000. Subsequent payments brought its total earnings to nearly double that sum, enough to leave a substantial balance after all debts of the dead author were paid.

Not until Dwight D. Eisenhower wrote his *Crusade in Europe* did the personal recollections of a chief executive earn more money than these produced by Ulysses S. Grant as the fruit of Mark Twain's first venture into publishing.

28

Mystery of the Warped and Twisted Genius from Meigs County

> *You are not permitted to kill a woman who has injured you, but nothing forbids you to reflect that she is growing older every minute. You are avenged 1,440 times a day.*
>
> —Epigrams
>
> Edible: *good to eat, and wholesome to digest, as a worm to a toad, a snake to a pig, a pig to a man, and a man to a worm.*
>
> Labor: *one of the processes by which A acquires property for B.*
>
> Marriage: *a community consisting of a master, a mistress, and two slaves, making in all, two.*
>
> —The Devil's Dictionary

These and scores of other witticisms from the pen of Ambrose Bierce suggest, but do not fully reveal, the nature of the Buckeye whose contemporaries described as being "obsessed with death and horror."

Born in a tiny cabin on Horse Cave Creek in 1842, the tenth of thirteen children, Ambrose Bierce was raised on a hard-scrabble farm in Indiana to which his family migrated in the vain hope of improving their lot. Working from sunup to sundown before the age of six, he had a meager education which he supplemented by reading available books.

When the Civil War began, he enlisted as a private in the Ninth Indiana Infantry, which was attached to the Army of the Ohio. A roll call of the battles in which he participated reveals the geographical moves of the Army of the Ohio: Shiloh, Corinth, Stones River, Chickamauga, Lookout Mountain, Missionary Ridge, Franklin, and Nashville, Tennessee. He was seriously wounded at Kennesaw Mountain and walked every mile of Sherman's March to the Sea, ending the war as a lieutenant.

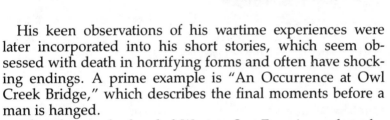

Maj. Gen. Don Carlos Buell, a native of Lowell and commander of the Army of the Ohio, brought the 9th Indiana infantry into his forces. [J. C. BUTTRE ENGRAVING]

His keen observations of his wartime experiences were later incorporated into his short stories, which seem obsessed with death in horrifying forms and often have shocking endings. A prime example is "An Occurrence at Owl Creek Bridge," which describes the final moments before a man is hanged.

After the war he headed West to San Francisco where he found work in the U.S. mint. Wanting to become a writer, he knew he first must master the mechanics of his trade—grammar, spelling, and punctuation. That he did so is a testamonial to his stubborn streak and the uncanny speed at which he learned.

Soon he began contributing to periodicals, then became an editor, and was considered the literary arbiter of the West Coast, but he took time out for an unsuccessful mining stint in the Dakota Territory. This was followed by a move to London where he wrote for magazines, edited material for the exiled French empress Eugénie. In England he was dubbed "Bitter Bierce."

In 1877 he joined the staff of William Randolph Hearst's San Francisco *Examiner,* with which he was associated as writer and columnist for twenty years before the paper sent

Shiloh log chapel near Pittsburgh Landing, Tennessee, named the battle in which Bierce said Confederate bayonets killed many Union soldiers who were stark naked and defenseless. [FRANK LESLIE'S ILLUSTRATED WEEKLY]

him to Washington, D.C., as its correspondent in 1896.

A cynical, misanthropic man who separated from his wife, lost two sons, and broke many friendships, he translated his attitudes into his satiric, witty writings where he attacked those he considered to be frauds, bores, or dishonest and pompous individuals. His targets ranged from clergymen to politicians. Most widely remembered today for the collection of brief and usually cynical "definitions" that make up the *Devil's Dictionary* (1906), he considered his best work to fall into the category now known as science fiction. The title of some of his books hint at their contents: *Cobwebs from an Empty Skull*, *The Dance of Death*, and *Fantastic Fables*. When admirers managed to gather up nearly everything he had published in newspapers and magazines, his *Collected Works* (1909–12) ran to twelve volumes. Many who have studied compare him with Edgar Allan Poe. Others have insisted that he was more like Bret Harte than Poe.

*   *   *

This self-taught genius whose handling of words was unique in quality was a top literary celebrity when he took action that shocked many.

Most of 1913 was spent in a long journey that took him to many of the battlefields at which he had heard cannon boom and bullets whine. Then he announced that in keeping with his denouncement of the Spanish-American War, he intended to fight against American imperialism. He would go to Mexico, find and join the forces of Pancho Villa, and help the leader known in Washington as "the bandit."

Ambrose Bierce is known to have entered Mexico from El Paso some time in November. From there he went to Chihuahua, where he wrote a letter filled with ecstasy at the certainty he would soon join Pancho Villa at Ojinaga. There the trail vanishes; when and where and under what circumstances the international celebrity died, no one knows.

Some who knew him well were positive that, plagued as always by fearful attacks of asthma, he planned his final journey as a suicide mission. That theory is strengthened by lines in a letter to a friend in which he exclaimed, "Bah! I'd hate to die between sheets, and, God willing, I won't."

Decades of inquiry have failed to solve the mystery of his disappearance. Describing his plan to cross South America after giving his best for what he considered "the Mexican brand of freedom," he had mused:

> Naturally, it is possible—even probable—that I shall not return. These be "strange countries," in which things happen; that is why I am going. And I am seventy-one.

The mysterious end of this strange man is heightened by remembering that he won fame in 1873 by the publication of a volume titled, *The Fiend's Delight*.

29

Victoria Woodhull's Visions Began at Age Three

"Some mighty queer things are going on at the gristmill."

"What's Buck Claflin up to now?"

"It's not him, this time. Seems that his Victoria spends a lot of time talking with her dead sisters."

"Don't know anything about Victoria. How old is she?"

"Buck says she's just turned three. He believes her, he says. Don't think I want to get caught messing around their place after dark."

Of the men gathered in the only general store in that part of Licking County, just two had caught glimpses of the girl born in 1838. To most pioneers in Hiram, "the Claflin tribe" constituted outsiders with whom no one liked to have contact.

Little Victoria, who had no idea that she was considered strange by adults in the crossroads settlement, talked constantly about her visions. Her mother, who had a smattering of understanding about mesmerism, was sympathetic. Buck was too busy at the grist mill to pay much attention to his daughter, but he didn't seem surprised when she told about being visited by "a tall fellow wearing a thin white shawl."

Later analysts concluded that the stranger from the spirit world was Demosthenes, the Greek orator. Whatever he was, according to Victoria he promised, "You're dirt poor now, but some day you will live in a fine mansion. From it, you will become ruler of your country."

When the gristmill went up in flames on a quiet night, nearby settlers were sympathetic at first. Then they learned that it was heavily insured, in a day when few on the Ohio frontier even knew what fire insurance was. Accused of arson, Buck Claflin fled but left his family behind. Neighbors who preferred they not be close by collected enough money to send them to Mount Gilead, where they stayed briefly before moving to Columbus.

By the time she was fifteen, Victoria was described as "looking a lot like a grown woman—pretty, too." She married Dr. Canning Woodhull, and they had two children. However, her ties with her family were so strong that she spent months of every year helping Buck to sell an Elixir of Life that he had concocted. Labels bore the portrait of Victoria's younger sister, Tennessee, described as "a raving beauty." Small Hebern, their brother, called himself a cancer doctor and offered to cure just about anything—for a price.

Fanning out from a new base in Cincinnati, the family medicine show covered much of the state. Profits ran high enough to pay for an occasional trip to Chicago, which gave Victoria and Tennessee a taste of life in a big city. Approaching age thirty and divorced from Woodhull, Victoria told her sister that the two of them had been called to New York in a vision.

Buck and several of his other offspring took the message from the spirit world so seriously that they decided to accompany them. After they reached New York in 1868, the family became very busy helping the sisters who now billed themselves as clairvoyants.

Long before Pearl Gray decided to adopt his name without making the change legal, Tennessee was calling herself Tennie C. Claflin. When a man arrived for a reading in an elegant hansom cab driven by a servant in livery, she made herself available for his every want. It is said that's how Cornelius Vanderbilt became involved with the sisters whose education was strictly from the school of hard knocks.

Vanderbilt gave them advice about when to buy and when to sell stocks, so they accumulated money enough to launch *Woodhull and Claflin's Weekly* in 1870. As its publisher, Victoria became the first woman to control a nationally circulated newspaper. That same year the sisters also became the first

Successful investments made under the guidance of Cornelius Vanderbilt caused Victoria and Tennie C. to be portrayed as "driving the bulls and bears of Wall Street." [NEW YORK EVENING TELEGRAPH (FEBRUARY 18, 1870)]

women to own a stock brokerage firm, which was situated near Wall Street.

Most women of the 1870s would have been more than satisfied with such triumphs. Victoria might have been had not her childhood spirit guide continued to visit her and remind her that one day she'd rule her nation, which is why she set her sight on the presidency. A deterrent in gaining support from the emerging women's rights groups was her stand on other more controversial issues. Articles in her newspaper rejected conventional marriage and advocated free love combined with communal management of children and property. However, women's groups aligned themselves with her after she performed a remarkable political feat.

With the help of General Benjamin Butler of Civil War fame, Victoria did something never before attempted: she petitioned Congress to protect women in their right to vote.

This privilege, argued Victoria, already belonged to them by virtue of the Fourteenth and Fifteenth Amendments to the Constitution. After the presentation was received on December 21, 1870, Representative George W. Julian of Indiana had the document sent to the House Committee of the Judiciary. John S. Harris of Louisiana referred it to the Senate as well.

On the following day, Victoria was the keynote speaker at the National Woman Suffrage Association's third annual convention in Washington. According to the New York *Herald*, "other speeches were made, but once Mrs. Woodhull had spoken, the rest were not heeded."

Butler's prestige was sufficient to bring Victoria before the House Judiciary Committee to testify on January 11. No other woman had been permitted to make an appearance

Appalled that the Weekly *advocated "free love," opponents of the movement for women's suffrage dubbed Victoria "Mrs. Satan."* [LIBRARY OF CONGRESS]

there on behalf of any cause. The men listened with interest, then effectively killed consideration of the measure by sending it to a committee that seldom functioned.

By November 1872, Victoria was sufficiently credible to those leading the fight for women's suffrage to be nominated as candidate for the presidency by the Equal Rights Party, becoming the first woman in the United States to run for that office. Judge David K. Cartter of Cincinnati, who had clinched the Republican nomination for Abraham Lincoln at Chicago in 1860, put her name in nomination. The slot for vice president was offered to the noted black activist, the former slave, Frederick Douglass, who declined to run.

Led by Susan B. Anthony, sixteen women in Rochester, New York, succeeded in registering to vote. They may have voted for Victoria, but her national support was so low that the votes she garnered in the presidential election were never officially tallied.

Concurrent with Victoria's political campaign, the sisters continued to make news with their *Weekly* publication. It printed the first English translation of Marx and Engels's *Communist Manifesto*, then provoked a national scandal by exposing alleged adultery on the part of the Reverend Henry Ward Beecher. The sisters were indicted for sending improper material through the mail but were acquitted the following year.

After the sudden death of Cornelius Vanderbilt it was found that his will provided substantial support for the work of Victoria and Tennie C. Relatives contested the will and the issue was settled out of court for an undisclosed sum, which was sufficient for them to make a trip to England. There Victoria married a wealthy banker, John Biddulph Martin, and Tennie C. married Francis Cook, a wealthy merchant and art collector, thus becoming Lady Cook. Both moved in the best social circles. Victoria published a journal devoted to eugenics and patronized the emerging aviation industry shortly before World War I.

Victoria returned to the United States only once. She came in obedience to instructions from her spirit guide and counselor who told her that on the twentieth anniversary of her

Woodhull & Claflin's Weekly, *priced at five cents, achieved a circulation of 20,000 and obtained most of its revenue from front-page advertisements.* [AUTHOR'S COLLECTION]

Gen. Benjamin F. Butler, portrayed by noted cartoonist Thomas Nast as "the Lone Fisherman," was the only prominent political leader willing to espouse Victoria Woodhull's cause.
[AUTHOR'S COLLECTION]

bid for the presidency she should try again. Many newspapers reported her announcement that she had come in order, as chief executive, "to launch a system of education which will waken people to the responsibility of creating a race of gods instead of inferior human beings."

Victoria gave interviews and distributed press releases much as she had in 1872. This time, however, she lacked the power base of even a meager political party. Having misunderstood Demosthenes or having failed to follow his instructions to the letter, the visionary woman from Ohio received not a single vote. Preparing for her second attempt to gain the White House, she failed to meet requirements for registration and was prevented from voting for herself.

Index